ALABAMA STUDIO
SEWING PATTERNS

ALABAMA STUDIO

SEWING PATTERNS

A GUIDE TO CUSTOMIZING A HAND-STITCHED ALABAMA CHANIN WARDROBE

Natalie Chanin

Photographs by Rinne Allen, Robert Rausch, and Abraham Rowe
Illustrations by Sun Young Park

ABRAMS | NEW YORK

CONTENTS

INTRODUCTION

When I started working on our first book, *Alabama Stitch Book*, in 2004, it never occurred to me that an entirely new arm of Alabama Chanin, today called The School of Making, was about to take shape. Back then, a book was a simple way to open-source our designs and techniques and help preserve American stitching traditions. *Alabama Stitch Book* and the two books that followed it—*Alabama Studio Style* and *Alabama Studio Sewing + Design*—resonated in the maker and sustainable design communities; sewers all over the world began to work in the Alabama Chanin style.

This style, as I've written before, was inspired by my grandmothers, who showed me how to make everything from biscuits to lace, and who lived their lives in a modest but beautiful way. My mother's mother once explained to me that she had two dresses growing up: one to wear during the week and another for her Sunday best. As times changed, her wardrobe expanded, but she maintained this spirit of thrift in the best possible way. Everything she put in her home mattered, from her homemade breads to her cross-stitched pillowcases. How a table looked was as important to her as how the meal on the table tasted. I remember watching her sew dresses from scratch and alter store-bought ones so they fit exactly as she liked. When styles changed, she would make gentle adjustments, keeping her garments current through years of fashion seasons. She would shorten a hemline, then create a belt with the leftover fabric, change a sleeve, or, in the end, cut a garment apart altogether to harvest the fabric for another idea. The result was a closet of garments that she loved and wanted to wear again and again. That closet and her dresses became the foundation of my childhood, my adult imagination, and my work as a designer.

But what seemed so simple and like second nature to my grandmother is daunting for many of us today. With home economics classes rare and throwaway fashion the norm, we are losing practical sewing skills and, as a result, many people have never actually had the pleasure of wearing a garment that fits really well. The fact is that much of what we call fashion today is designed to look best on extremely young and slim bodies, bodies that represent a contemporary cultural ideal but not the reality of most women. And although there are some great companies offering a range of size options, there are also impossible sizing gaps that just cannot be met by the ready-to-wear market.

As a designer, I have learned firsthand that fit is by far one of the most challenging subjects to address. There are just so many different body types and sizes, ranging from round to pear, petite to large, and everything in between. Back in 2000, when I started this venture, I was designing garments that I wanted to wear in sizes and styles that suited my forty-year-old body, which was—and still is—more round than slim. Today I am older (and a few pounds heavier) than I was when those patterns were made, but the styling of those original garments still feels flattering to me; I just choose a size (or two) larger. Over the years my team and I have added many more styles to our collections, and we have tried to accommodate many different body types.

However, not surprisingly, since we began making our patterns available in our books, we have received requests to expand our offerings. Some people want looser styles; some people want a wider selection of sleeve options; others want more sizes. We are pleased to offer more garments here, but because we know we cannot please everyone, we are also sharing our techniques for altering our garments so that you can customize as you like (just as my grandmothers did). The truth is that sometimes if you want a garment to really and truly fit and suit you, you have to take the power of creating or altering it into your own hands. You have to be willing to nip in a waistline here, shorten a hemline there and, sometimes, start from scratch.

In Chapter 1, you will find the new garment patterns and a range of variations. The garments from our previous books can also be found in this chapter and, for the first time, all of the patterns for all of the garments in this book and the three earlier ones are included on a disk attached to the inside back cover. In Chapter 2, we present our favorite techniques for altering the fit and styles of our garments. To my mind, this is the heart of the book. This is what will make our patterns—as well as other commercially available patterns—truly customizable. And in Chapter 3, we present an overview of the supplies and tools we like to use in the design and sewing of our garments, along with instructions for some of our favorite embellishment techniques. This section is not intended as a substitute for the instructions offered in our other books but does provide the basic information you need to create our garments.

It has been such a beautiful and inspiring journey to the creation of this book. I have learned so much along the way, and I am grateful for all of the readers and followers who have found passion in doing things the Alabama Chanin way.

Natalie
Florence, Alabama

The idea for this book was born during a workshop in Hudson, New York. The conversation turned to fit and customization, and as hard as I tried to convince everyone they could adapt our patterns to suit their bodies and styles on their own, they insisted they wanted guidance. I realized then that I might be taking for granted the expertise at our studio and that it would be helpful for us to document our fit and customization techniques. Everyone at the workshop also asked for more garment patterns. So, to start, I present three new patterns that can be used to create many garments, plus all of the garment patterns from our previous books. Being able to mix and match and adapt our pieces to create a versatile wardrobe has always been integral to my design philosophy, so it was important to me to present everything together here. I've consolidated the instructions to avoid unnecessary repetition between this book and the others and I've introduced new variations. If you are new to sewing in the Alabama Chanin style, read our instructions and the glossary (see page 127) carefully. Our methods don't always follow general standards as they are specific to hand-sewing cotton jersey.

New Patterns for This Book

For the first time here, we are offering home sewers our patterns for our A-Line Dress/Tunic/Top, for our Classic Coat/Jacket/Cardigan, and for our Wrap Skirt. These garments are favorites among our staff and customers. The A-Line set of garments, starting on page 16, in all its lengths and variations, has been my "uniform" for several years. I have basic, unembellished versions and also elaborately embellished ones that I mix and match for all occasions. The Classic Coat, Jacket, and Cardigan on page 30 have been Alabama Chanin favorites since the pattern was developed in 2007. For many of our clients, these are go-to pieces for work, travel, and everyday use. Finally, the Wrap Skirt on page 36 is a new style that has quickly become popular. With my larger hips, I never before felt comfortable in a wrap; however, this piece works for my figure type as well as for others.

As with the rest of the garments in this and all our books, these new patterns call for working with our fabric of choice, 100-percent organic cotton jersey. In Part 3 (starting on page 127), you can learn more about this fabric and the construction and embellishment techniques that we find work best.

A-Line Dress/Tunic/Top

This pattern has become our core uniform at the store and café. It has a V-neck and shaped side seams to give a snugger fit around the bustline, and it flares out just under the bust. Comfortable and feminine, the pattern includes four lengths: top, tunic, dress, and long dress.

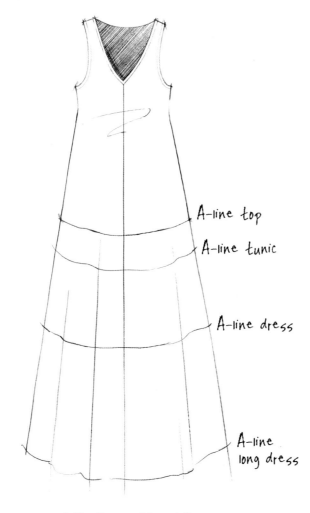

A-line top
A-line tunic
A-line dress
A-line long dress

A-Line Dress and its variations

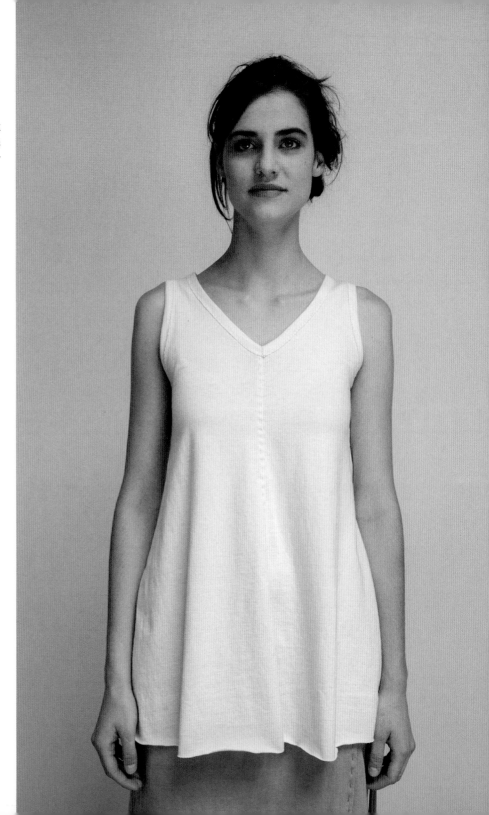

LONG A-LINE DRESS

This long version of our A-Line Dress is great as a summer caftan in a single layer of our lightweight cotton-jersey fabric or as the basis of a heavily embroidered evening dress in a double layer of our medium-weight fabric. The dress measures approximately 55" (1.4 m) from the shoulder to the hem.

A-LINE DRESS

This dress has become an Alabama Chanin classic since it is so versatile and fits a wide variety of body shapes. The dress measures approximately 39" (97.5 cm) from the shoulder to the hem.

A-LINE TUNIC

With a length between the A-Line Dress and A-Line Top, the A-Line Tunic works well with many pieces from an existing wardrobe. Women with great legs like to wear this as a mini-dress; it can also be paired with yoga pants for a workout piece or with a straight skirt and heels for days in the office or nights out. The tunic measures approximately 29" (72.5 cm) from the shoulder to the hem.

A-LINE TOP

This short version of the A-Line Dress looks great over pants or a skirt and under the Cardigan (see page 30). The top measures about 25" (63.5 cm) from the shoulder to the hem.

55" (1.4 m) 39" (97.5 cm) 29" (72.5 cm) 25" (63.5 cm)

All of these pieces can be shortened or lengthened easily at the bottom edge (see page 112) or at the waistline by making an internal alteration (see page 114).

A-Line Dress/Tunic/Top Master Pattern

The master pattern for the A-Line Dress/Tunic/Top on the CD included with this book can be used to make the A-Line Dress and all of its variations—Long A-Line Dress, A-Line Dress, A-Line Tunic, and A-Line Top. (See the chart on page 174 for the yardage needed for each of these garments.)

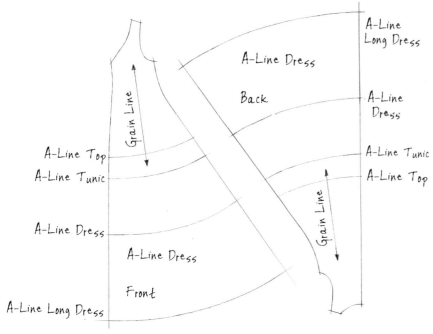

A-Line Master Pattern pieces

A-Line Dress/Tunic/Top Instructions

SUPPLIES

Basic sewing supplies listed on page 128

A-Line Dress pattern printed from this book's CD

60"- (1.5-m-) wide light- or medium-weight cotton-jersey fabric (see page 130) in one color, for top layer (see chart on page 174 for yardage needed)

60"- (1.5-m-) wide light- or medium-weight cotton-jersey fabric in a second color, for backing layer (optional)

The instructions below are specifically for the A-Line Dress (either single- or double-layer); however, they can also be used for the Long A-Line Dress, A-Line Tunic, and A-Line Top as well as for the Short/Long Fitted Dress, Fitted Top, and Fitted Tunic.

1. Prepare and Cut Pattern

Print out the A-Line Dress pattern from the CD (see page 86), and use paper scissors to cut the printed pattern to your desired size (see also "Mixing and Matching Pattern Sizes" on page 88), cutting as close as possible to the black cutting line. The pattern has two pieces—a front panel and a back panel—with a ¼" (6 mm) seam allowance built into all the pattern edges.

2. Cut Top-Layer Pattern Pieces

Lay out your top-layer fabric flat, and then fold the fabric's width in half across the grain (see page 135), with wrong sides together and the edges aligned, creating two layers. Since these pattern pieces can become very wide as they get longer, you will save fabric by laying them out as shown at left.

Place the A-Line Dress pattern front on top of the folded yardage, making sure the pattern and fabric grain lines (see page 135) run in the same direction. Use tailor's chalk to trace around the pattern's edges, remove the pattern, and cut out the traced pattern with fabric scissors, cutting just inside the chalked line to remove it entirely. (Note that we prefer holding or weighting the pattern to pinning it on the fabric, which, in the case of cotton jersey, often skews the fabric and makes the cutting uneven.) You will now have two front pieces. Repeat this step on the remaining yardage with your A-Line Dress back, which will give you two back pieces, for a total of four pieces for the garment's top layer.

3. Cut Backing-Layer Pattern Pieces (optional)

To make a double-layer garment (which you will need if you are planning to embellish heavily), lay out the backing fabric flat, and fold it in half as you did with the top-layer fabric, with wrong sides together and edges aligned, to create two layers. Then repeat Step 2, using your cut front and back top-layer pieces as pattern guides, and cut two backing-layer pieces. You will now have four front pieces and four back dress pieces.

4. Baste Neckline and Armholes

To ensure the neckline and armholes do not stretch while you are constructing, use a single strand of all-purpose thread to baste (see page 136) the neckline and armhole edges of each cut piece.

5. Add Stenciling (optional)

If you'd like to stencil your garment, refer to the overview on page 146 of this book. Add the stenciling as desired on the right side of the A-Line Dress's top layer only, and let the image dry thoroughly.

6. Pin Pattern's Top and Backing Layers (optional)

If you are making a double-layer garment, align each cut top-layer piece on the corresponding backing-layer piece, with both fabrics facing right side up, and pat the layers into place with your fingertips so that their edges match. Securely pin together the two layers of each piece, being sure to scatter your pins across the face of the project piece, as shown on the skirt on page 39.

7. Add Embellishment (optional)

Complete all the embellishments that you want to add to your project (see pages 136–161). If you are adding beading, be sure to avoid beading in the ¼" (6 mm) seam allowance.

8. Prepare for Construction

After completing the embellishment, choose how you want to work your seams from the list of options on pages 144–145. When pinning knit seams for construction, it is important to follow a method we call "pinning the middle": Start by pinning the top of your seam, and follow by pinning the bottom of your seam. After pinning both top and bottom, place one pin in the middle between the two initial pins. Continue by pinning in the middle of each set of pins, as shown in the illustration on page 20, until your seam is securely pinned and ready to sew. Repeat the process for the dress's two back panels, pinning them together at the center back.

9. Construct Dress

Thread your needle with button craft thread, "love your thread," and knot off (see pages 132–133). Using a straight stitch (see page 136), sew the pinned pieces together, starting at the top edge of the center front and stitching ¼" (6 mm) from the fabric's cut edges down to the bottom edge. Be sure to begin and end the seam by wrap-stitching (see page 144) its edges to secure them. Fell (see page 145) each seam by folding over the seam allowances to one side and topstitching them ⅛" (3 mm) from the cut edges (down the center of the seam allowances), using a straight stitch and wrap-stitching the seam. Repeat this process to sew the center-back seam.

Next pin the shoulder seams, with the raw edges aligned, and sew the seams, following the instructions above for sewing the front and back panels. Note that you can either leave the shoulder seams floating (see page 144) or fold the allowances toward the back and fell them down the center. Pin the constructed front and back panels together at the side seams, with right sides together, and follow the instructions above for sewing the panels together.

10. Bind Neckline and Armholes

Use the rotary cutter, cutting mat, and large plastic ruler to cut 1¼"- (3 cm-) wide strips of leftover fabric across the grain to use for binding the neckline and armholes. You will need two strips, each approximately 55" (1.4 m), for the binding. Use your iron to press each binding strip in half lengthwise, with the wrong sides together, being careful not to stretch the fabric while pressing it. To bind the neckline, you will first make a miter at the mid-point of the binding before applying the binding to the neckline (see page 22). Then you will apply the mitered point over the neckline's center-front V, work the binding around each side of the neckline, and finish at the center-back.

To bind and finish each armhole, repeat the binding process, skipping the instructions for making and applying a mitered V-shaped binding at the center-front V-neck. After permanently sewing the neckline and armhole bindings in place with a stretch stitch (see page 138), remove or simply break the basting stitches (encased inside the binding) by pulling gently to snap the thread. If some of the basting stitches remain embedded in the binding, leave them in place since the thread is broken and the remaining stitches will not restrict the fabric's stretch.

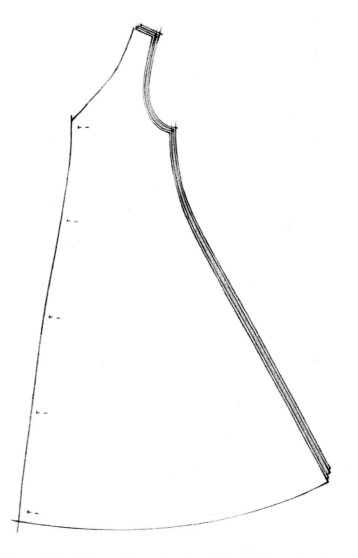

When pinning knit seams for construction, pin top, bottom, and center, then in the middle of each set of pins until your seam is secure.

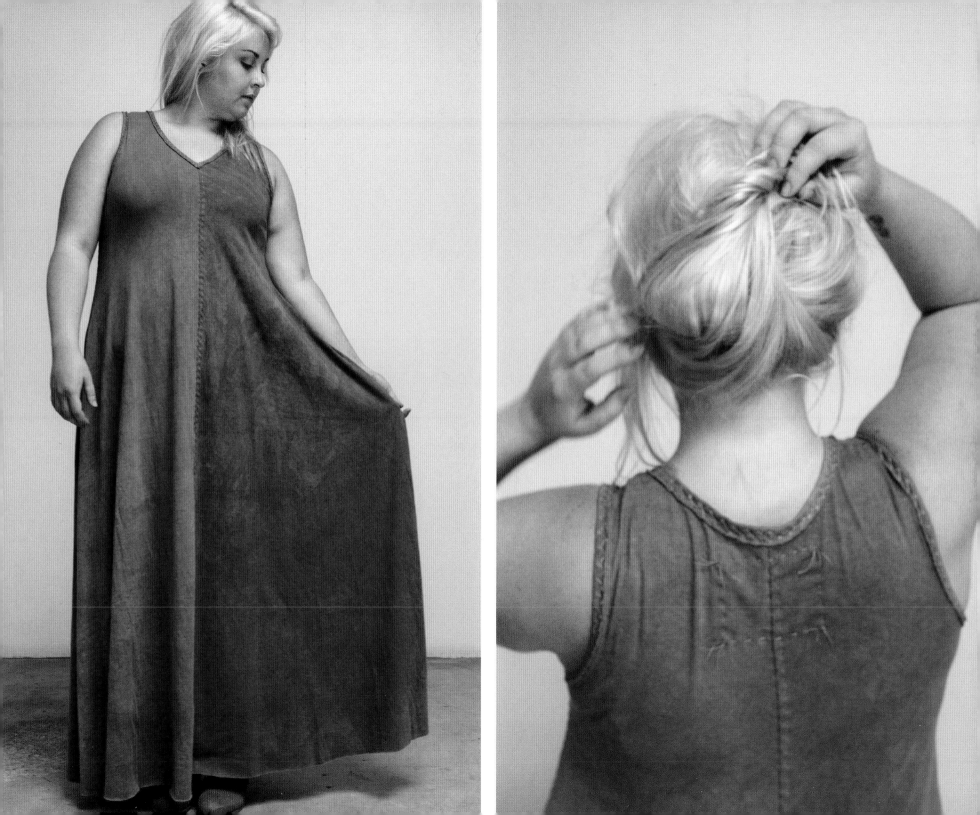

CREATING MITERED RIBBING BINDING FOR A-LINE DRESS/TUNIC/TOP

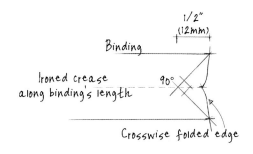

Fold binding and mark V-shape.

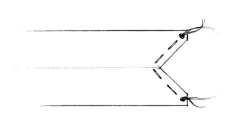

Stitch V-shape, clip excess from "V," and turn right side out.

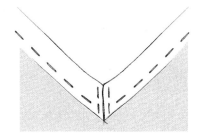

Place mitered "V" at center-front neckline, baste binding around neckline, and sew it in place.

Open the pressed binding flat, and then fold it in half crosswise, with right sides together and the short edges aligned. Starting at one edge of the binding, stitch to the fold line and then back to the other edge, sewing a 90-degree V-shape whose point is ½" (12 mm) from the binding's folded edge, and knotting off at the other edge. Clip the excess fabric from V-shape, leaving a ¼" (6 mm) seam allowance.

Turn the binding right side out; re-fold it with wrong sides together; and place the mitered V at the neckline's center-front V, folding the strip along the fold line and over the neckline's raw edge. Start basting the binding in place with all-purpose thread, encasing the neckline's raw edge inside the binding (note that the binding's raw edges will show). You will remove this basting thread at the end of the binding process. Add a new binding strip, as needed, as you work around the neckline's edge to the center back, overlapping the short raw edges of the existing and new binding strips by about ½" (12 mm).

When you reach the center-back point, overlap the binding's short raw edges by about ½" (12 mm) to finish the binding, and trim away any excess binding. To permanently sew the binding in place, use the stretch stitch (see page 138) of your choice to sew through all layers down the middle of the binding.

Design Variation

DEEP V-BACK EVENING DRESS

Use this variation on the A-Line Dress to create an evening dress with a deep V-back. The dress shown here has a 12"- (30.5-cm-) deep V at the center-back neck, which is created by drawing a straight line from the shoulder seam at the neckline to the desired depth of the V (see the ilustration below). Trim the V-section of the pattern piece away, and follow the instructions beginning on page 18 for the A-Line Dress. At center back, follow the instructions in Step 10 and on page 22 to create the V-shaped mitered binding, and continue with the binding by overlapping additional strips as needed.

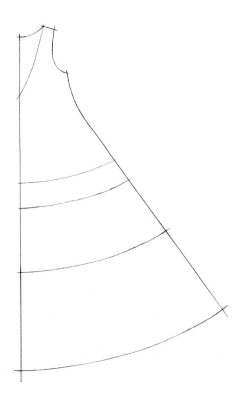

Altering pattern's back neck

Clean-Finishing Seams

We rarely finish our hems or seam allowances; instead, we leave the edges raw because the cotton-jersey fabric does not ravel. After a few washings, the jersey edges roll, but the fabric does not run, snag, or tear. When we do not want to leave a raw edge, we clean-finish the edge, meaning that we stitch the seam allowances to encase them on the inside of the garment. To make a clean-finished seam:

1. Place your cut garment pieces with the right sides together and the edges aligned.
2. Stitch your seam with a ¼" (6 mm) seam allowance, as described in your pattern instructions.
3. Press your seam allowances open.
4. Turn your fabric panels so that the wrong sides face together and the stitched seam allowances are hidden between the two layers of fabric, and press the folded edge.
5. Topstitch ⅛" (3 mm) from the folded edge with a straight stitch to encase the seam permanently between the two garment panels, as shown in the illustration, and press.

Note that clean-finishing a seam can add bulk to the seam allowance. When making embellished garments with clean-finished seams, complete the clean finish before adding embellishments, then embellish right up to the clean-finished edge.

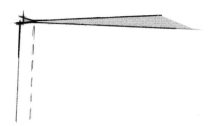

Stitch panels with right sides together.

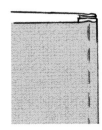

Turn panels right side out, press edge, and stitch again.

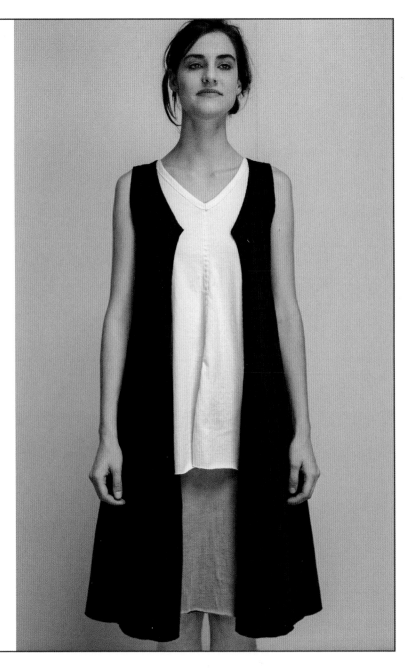

ADDING PIPING TO SEAMS

Sometimes we add piping to seams to accentuate them. In the A-Line Top shown here, we folded a ⅝" (15 mm) strip of contrasting fabric in half lengthwise and stitched it inside each seam so that just about ¼" (6 mm) shows. We've also added color blocking to highlight the piping. For more information about working with seams, see page 144.

Inside Floating Seam

Outside Floating Seam

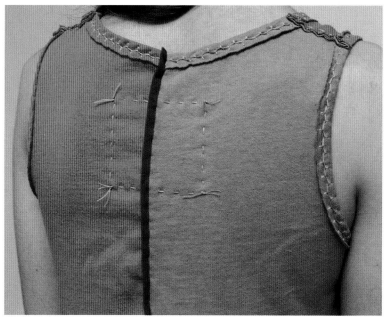

ADDING SIDE-SEAM POCKETS

We have included an optional side-seam pocket pattern on the CD at the back of this book. Deciding how high to insert the pockets in the side seam is a matter of personal preference. I prefer my pockets set a bit on the high side; others with longer arms may prefer a lower pocket. We have indicated an average pocket height on the A-line Dress pattern pieces, but you should raise or lower the pockets as you want. Set this pocket in each side-seam panel, and attach it, as shown, before pinning the front panels to the back panels in Step 9 on page 20.

1. Cut four side-seam pockets from your pattern piece in the color desired.

2. Determine how high you want to position your pocket, and match the pocket height on both side seams, on both the dress front and the dress back.

3. Attach each side-seam pocket to the corresponding pattern piece, with right sides together and the straight edges aligned.

4. Fold back each pocket, and fell your seam (see page 145) to the front of the garment's front pattern piece and to the back of the back pattern piece.

5. Align and pin the front garment panel to the back garment panel, with wrong sides together, and continue pinning the panels together around the side-seam pockets.

6. Sew the side seams, following all of the instructions for constructing your garment but stitching around the pinned side-seam pockets at the same time leaving the seam open across the pocket opening.

7. To reinforce the stress points where the pockets are attached, secure them with additional tacking stitches.

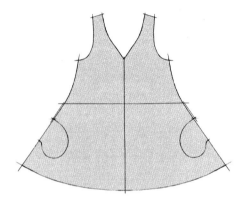

2. Match pocket height on each side.

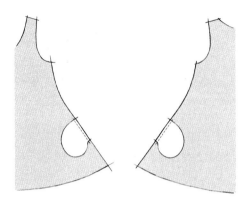

3. Attach pockets to corresponding pattern pieces.

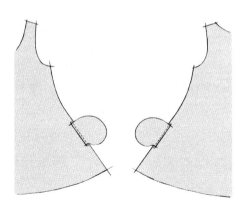

4. Fell pocket seams.

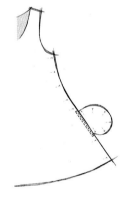

5. Pin garment's side and pocket seams.

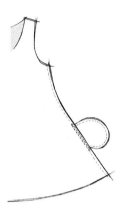

6. Sew side and pocket seams in one continuous pass.

7. Reinforce pocket's stress points by tacking them.

Classic Coat/Jacket/Cardigan

The Classic Coat, Jacket, and Cardigan have long been staples of our collections. Great for layering, they can be made double-layer for chilly weather and single-layer for warmer times.

Classic Coat and its variations

CLASSIC COAT

This classic shape makes a great year-round garment in its most basic version (or with slight embellishments) and can become a coveted statement piece with the addition of intricate embellishments. The coat measures approximately 37" (92.5 cm) from the shoulder to the hem.

MID-LENGTH CLASSIC JACKET

At a mid-length, this garment is sure to become one of your favorite all-around, everyday jackets. Add pockets both inside and out (see how to add patch pockets on page 63) for the perfect companion to everyday life and/or traveling. This version measures approximately 23" (57.5 cm) from the shoulder to the hem.

CLASSIC CARDIGAN

This cardigan is extremely versatile and can be used for everything from a bridal accessory to a suit jacket when paired with the Wrap Skirt on page 36. It measures approximately 19" (48 cm) from the shoulder to the hem.

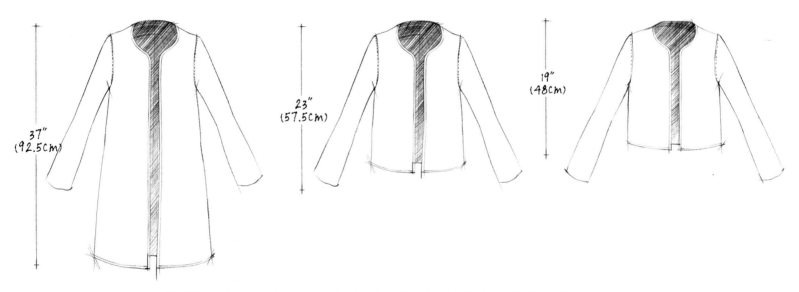

All of these pieces can be shortened or lengthened easily at the bottom edge by making a perimeter alteration (see page 112) or at the waistline by making an internal alteration (see page 114).

Classic Coat/Jacket/Cardigan Master Pattern

The master pattern for the Coat/Jacket/Cardigan on the book's CD can be used to make the Coat and the Jacket and Cardigan variations. (See the chart on page 174 for the yardage needed for each of these garments.)

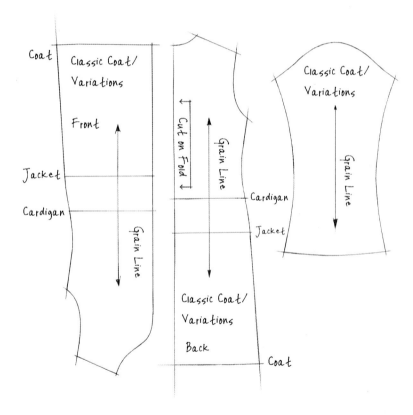

Classic Coat Master Pattern pieces

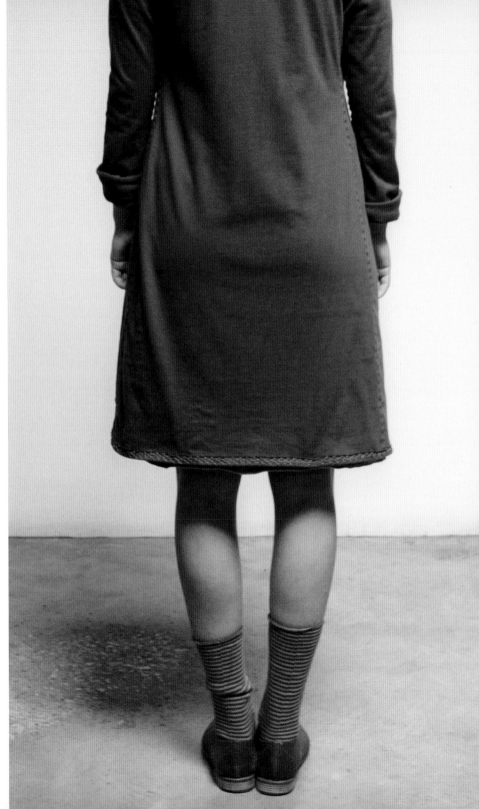

Classic Coat/Jacket/Cardigan Instructions

SUPPLIES

Basic sewing supplies listed on page 128

Classic Coat/Jacket/Cardigan pattern printed from this book's CD

60"- (1.5-m-) wide light- or medium-weight cotton-jersey fabric (see page 130) in one color, for top layer (see chart on page 174 for yardage needed)

60"- (1.5-m-) wide light- or medium-weight cotton-jersey fabric in a second color, for backing layer (optional)

The instructions below are specifically for the Classic Coat; however, they can also be followed for the Classic Jacket and Cardigan as well.

1. Prepare and Cut Pattern

Print out the Classic Coat pattern from the CD (see page 86), and use paper scissors to cut the pattern to your desired size (see also "Mixing and Matching Pattern Sizes" on page 88), cutting as close as possible to the black cutting line. The pattern has three pieces—a front panel, back panel, and sleeve—with a ¼" (6 mm) seam allowance built into all the pattern edges.

2. Cut Top-Layer Pattern Pieces

Lay out your top-layer fabric flat, and then fold the fabric's width in half with the grain (see page 135), with wrong sides together and the edges aligned, creating two layers. Place the Classic Coat pattern front on top of the folded yardage, making sure the pattern and fabric grain lines run in the same direction. (We like to hold or weight the pattern instead of pinning it on the fabric, which can skew the cotton jersey and make the cutting uneven.) Use tailor's chalk to trace around the pattern pieces' edges, remove the pattern, and use fabric scissors to cut out the traced pattern, cutting just inside the chalked line to remove it entirely. You will now have your two front pieces. Repeat this step on the remaining yardage with the Classic Coat sleeve and then with your Classic Coat back, positioning the back pattern piece on the fold to cut it out. This will give you a total of five pieces for the garment's top layer.

3. Cut Backing-Layer Pattern Pieces (optional)

If you want to make a double-layer garment, repeat Step 2, using your cut top-layer front, back, and sleeve pieces as pattern guides. Cut a total of five backing-layer pieces. You will now have four front pieces, two back pieces, and four sleeves, for a total of ten pieces.

4. Baste Neckline and Armholes

To ensure that the neckline and armholes on your cut fabric pieces do not stretch while you are constructing the coat, use a single strand of all-purpose thread to baste (see page 136) the neckline and armhole edges of each cut piece, as noted on the pattern pieces.

5. Stencil and Embellish (optional)

If you'd like to stencil or embellish your garment, follow Steps 5-7 for the A-Line Dress on page 18, using Step 6 only if you are making a double-layer garment.

6. Prepare for Construction

After completing any embellishment, choose how you want to work your seams from the list of options on pages 144–145. Begin constructing the Classic Coat by pinning the front and back panels together at the shoulders, with right sides together and the edges aligned.

7. Sew Shoulder Seams

Thread your needle, "love your thread," and knot off (see pages 132–133). Using a straight stitch (see page 136), stitch the pinned pieces together at the shoulder, starting at the top edge of the Coat's armhole, sewing ¼" (6 mm) from the fabric's cut edges across to the neckline, and beginning and ending the seam by wrap-stitching it (see page 144). Fell your seam by folding over the seam allowances towards the back of the Coat and topstitching the seam allowances ⅛" (3 mm) from the cut edges (down the center of the seam allowances), using a straight stitch and again wrap-stitching the beginning and end of the seam.

8. Add Sleeves

Pin the cut sleeves to the Coat's armholes, matching each sleeve's front armhole edge to the Coat's front and the sleeve's back armhole edge to the Coat's back. Pin the edges securely, working in any excess fabric with your pins. Thread your needle, "love your thread," and knot off. Using a straight stitch, sew the pinned pieces together at the armhole, wrap-stitching the seam. Note that you can either leave the seam floating (see page 144), or fold the seam allowances toward the sleeve and fell them down the center.

9. Sew Side Seams

Pin together the front, back, and sleeves at the side seams. Using a straight stitch, starting at the edge of the Coat's hem, wrap-stitch the edge, and sew together the side and sleeve seams in one continuous pass. Attaching the side and sleeve seams this way produces a better-fitting armhole than sewing the side seams and sleeves separately and then inserting the sleeves into the armholes.

10. Bind Neckline and Armholes

Use the rotary cutter, cutting mat, and clear plastic ruler to cut 1¼"- (3-cm-) wide strips of leftover fabric across the grain to use for binding the neckline and armholes. You will need a total of about three 55–60"- (1.4–1.5 m-) long cut strips for the binding. Use your iron to press each binding strip in half lengthwise, with the wrong sides together, being careful not to stretch the fabric while pressing it.

Starting at the Coat's center-back neckline edge, encase the garment's entire raw edge (the neckline, front edges, and bottom edge) inside the folded binding (note that the binding's raw edges will show), and baste the binding into place with an all-purpose thread, which you will remove at the end of the binding process. Add a new binding strip, as needed, by simply overlapping the existing and new strips' short raw edges by about ½" (12 mm) and stitching over the overlap. When you reach the center-back point again, overlap the binding's short raw edges by about ½" (12 mm) to finish the binding, trimming away any excess binding. To sew the binding in place permanently, use the stretch stitch of your choice (see pages 138–143) to stitch through all layers down the middle of the binding. Then remove or simply break the neckline and armhole basting stitches by pulling gently on one end of the thread. If some basting stitches remain embedded in the binding, you can leave them in place since the thread is broken, and the remaining stitches will not restrict the fabric's stretch.

ADDING GATHERED RUFFLES TO CLASSIC COAT/ JACKET/CARDIGAN

This technique can be used to add a ruffle to the hem of the Classic Coat or any of our other garments.

To make a gathered ruffle, begin by simply cutting a cotton-jersey rectangle to the desired width across the grain, approximately three times the length of the garment edge to which you want to attach the ruffle. If you need a longer rectangle than you cut above, cut another rectangle of the same width, and sew them together to create the needed length, following the seam-construction method of your choice (see page 144). Using all-purpose thread, sew a basting stitch across the rectangle's long top edge, and pull on the ends of the basting thread to gather up the fabric.

Pin the gathered ruffle to the outside hem of your finished garment, overlapping the garment's bottom edge with the ruffle's top edge by ½" (12 mm) and aligning the side seams. Both edges are left raw. Distribute and pin the gathers evenly around the hem. Once you have pinned the ruffle in place, baste the gathered ruffle to the garment. Then attach it permanently with the stretch or decorative stitch of your choice (see page 138). Remove the basting stitches.

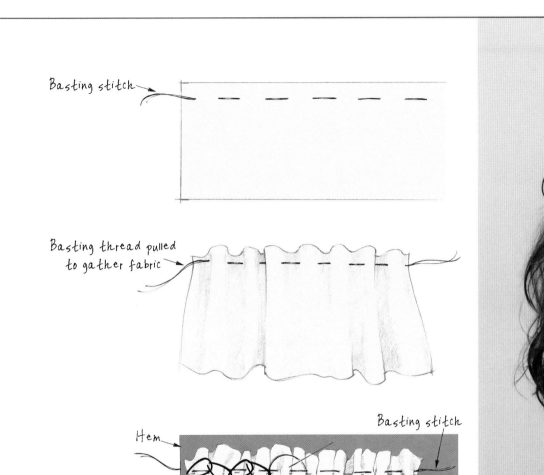

Basting stitch

Basting thread pulled to gather fabric

Basting stitch

Hem

Use stretch or decorative stitch to attach ruffle.

Wrap Skirt—Short/Classic/Long

Wrap skirts have been worn in cultures worldwide since the invention of fabric, with large swaths of cloth wrapped around the body and tied or pinned closed. And thanks to their comfort and versatility, wrap skirts have become a staple of modern-day dressing.

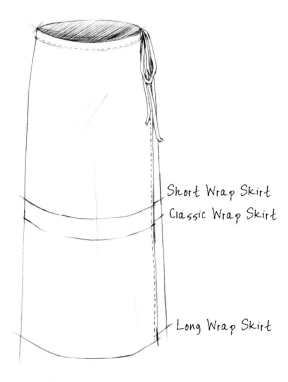

Short Wrap Skirt
Classic Wrap Skirt

Long Wrap Skirt

Wrap Skirt and its variations

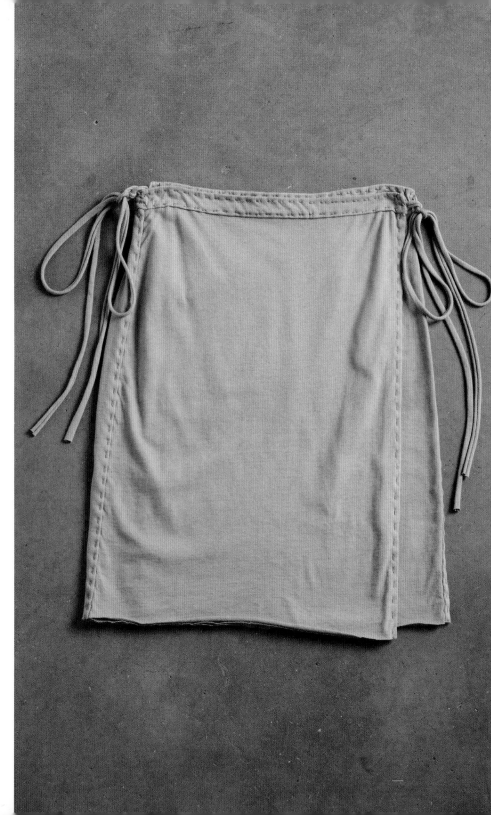

SHORT WRAP SKIRT

This short wrap style makes a great year-round garment; pair a basic version with a simple T-shirt, or add intricate embellishment to make a bolder fashion statement. This skirt measures approximately 21" (52.5 cm) from the waist to the hem.

CLASSIC WRAP SKIRT

This garment is destined to become one of your favorite all-around, everyday skirts. Add patch pockets (included with the Classic Coat pattern on the CD and great here too) to the sides, and it becomes even harder-working. This classic version measures approximately 26" (65 cm) from the waist to the hem.

LONG WRAP SKIRT

This skirt is extremely versatile and can be the basis of a bridal ensemble in white or the perfect beach cover-up in your favorite summer color. The skirt measures approximately 38" (95 cm) from the waist to the hem.

21"
(52.5 cm)

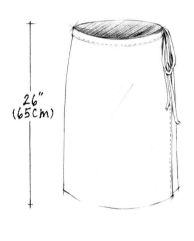

26"
(65 cm)

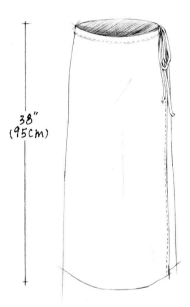

38"
(95 cm)

All of these pieces can be shortened or lengthened easily at the bottom edge by making a perimeter alteration (see page 112).

Wrap Skirt Master Pattern

The master pattern for the Wrap Skirt on the CD included with this book can be used to make the Wrap Skirt and all of its variations—short, classic, and long. (See the chart on page 174 for the yardage needed for the Wrap Skirt and each of its variations.)

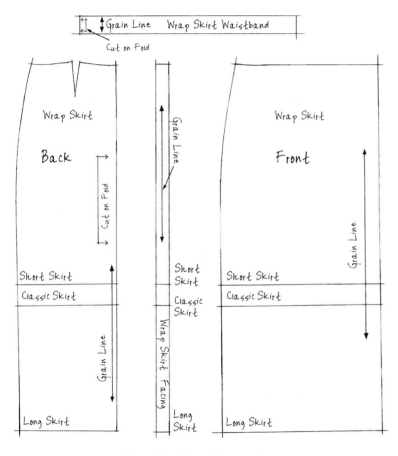

Wrap Skirt Master Pattern pieces

Wrap Skirt Instructions

SUPPLIES

Basic sewing supplies listed on page 128

Wrap Skirt pattern printed from this book's CD

60"- (1.5-m-) wide light- or medium-weight cotton-jersey fabric (see page 130) in one color, for top layer (see chart on page 174 for yardage needed)

60"- (1.5-m-) wide light- or medium-weight cotton-jersey fabric in a second color, for backing layer (optional)

1. Prepare and Cut Pattern

Print out the Wrap Skirt pattern from the CD (see page 86), and use paper scissors to cut the pattern to your desired size (see also "Mixing and Matching Pattern Sizes" on page 88), cutting as close as possible to the black cutting line. The pattern has four pieces—a front panel, back panel, front facing, and waistband—with a ¼" (6 mm) seam allowance built into all the pattern edges.

2. Cut Top-Layer Pattern Pieces

Lay out your top-layer fabric flat, and then fold the fabric's width in half with the grain (see page 135), with wrong sides together and the edges aligned, creating two layers. Then place the Wrap Skirt pattern front on top of the folded yardage, making sure the pattern and fabric grain lines run in the same direction. (We like to hold or weight the pattern instead of pinning it on the fabric, which can skew the cotton jersey and make the cutting uneven.) Use tailor's chalk to trace around the pattern pieces' edges, remove the pattern, and use fabric scissors to cut out the traced pattern, cutting just inside the chalked line to remove it entirely. You will now have your two front pieces. Repeat this step on the remaining yardage with your Wrap Skirt back (cut on the fold), facing, and waistband (also cut on the fold), which will give you a total of seven pieces for the garment's top layer: two fronts, one back on fold, two facings, and two waistbands.

3. Cut Backing-Layer Pattern Pieces (optional)

If you want to make a double-layer garment, repeat Step 2 for your front and back pieces only, using your cut top-layer front and back pieces as pattern guides. Cut three backing-layer pieces. You will now have a total of ten pieces: four fronts, two backs, two facings, and two waistbands (be sure to cut all the facings and waistbands out of the top-layer color).

4. Baste Waistband

To ensure that the waistline on your cut-fabric pieces does not stretch while you construct the skirt, use a single strand of all-purpose thread to baste (see page 136) the waistline edges of each cut piece, as noted on the pattern.

5. Add Stenciling (optional)

If you'd like to stencil your garment, refer to page 146. Add the desired stenciling on the right side of the Wrap Skirt's top layer only, and let the image dry thoroughly.

6. Pin Pattern's Top and Backing Layers (for double-layer garment, optional)

Align each cut top-layer piece on the corresponding backing-layer piece, with both fabrics facing right side up, and pat the layers into place with your fingertips so that their edges match. Securely pin together the two layers of each piece, being sure to scatter your pins across the face of the project piece (see illustration below).

Scattered pins holding cut top
and backing layers in place

7. Add embellishment (optional)

Complete all the embellishments that you want to add to your project. If you are adding beading, be sure to avoid beading in the ¼" (6 mm) seam allowance.

8. Prepare for Construction

Once you have completed your embellishment, begin constructing the skirt by sewing your darts. Pin the dart with right sides together (or, if you want to make the seams visible on the garment's right side, position the cut pieces with wrong sides together) and using the method of "pinning the middle" (see page 19). Using a ruler and tailor's chalk or a disappearing ink pen, draw a line starting at the skirt's top edge and ¼" (6 mm) from the dart's cut edge, and reduce the width of the seam allowance to ¹⁄₁₆" (2 mm) as you reach the dart's apex, or at the fullest part of the curve you are fitting (see page 103). Thread your needle, "love your thread," and knot off (see pages 132–133). Starting at the skirt's top edge, begin sewing your dart with a wrap stitch (see page 144) and construct your dart with a running stitch that follows your drawn line, finishing with a wrap stitch.

9. Construct Skirt

Pin your front and back panels together at the side seams with right sides together and edges aligned (or, if you want to make the seams visible on the garment's right side, position the cut pieces with wrong sides together), and use the method of "pinning the middle." Thread your needle, "love your thread," and knot off. Using a straight stitch, sew the pinned pieces together starting at the top edge of the skirt's waistline and stitching ¼" (6 mm) from the fabric's cut edges down to the bottom edge. Be sure to begin and end each seam by wrap-stitching its edges. Leave seams floating (see page 144), or fell your seams by stitching down the center of the seam allowances, using a straight stitch and wrap-stitching the beginning and end of each seam to secure it.

10. Add Facing to Front Panels

Pin your cut facing piece to the Wrap Skirt front panel, with right sides together and the edges aligned. Thread your needle, "love your thread," and knot off. Using a straight stitch, sew the pinned pieces together, starting at the top edge of the center front and stitching ¼" (6 mm) from the fabric's cut edges down to the bottom edge. Be sure to begin and end the seam by wrap-stitching its edges to secure them. Once you have constructed this seam, gently steam the seam open with an iron, and then fold the facing back to create a clean-finished

seam that encases the seam allowances (see page 145), and pin it into place. Using a straight stitch, topstitch through all of the layers ¼" (6 mm) from the front edge to secure the facing in place.

11. Add Waistband

To add the waistband, start by placing the two cut waistbands with right sides together and the edges aligned, and begin stitching at the short end, and then sew across top of band and the other short end, wrap-stitching at both ends of the seam. Turn the waistband right side out, and press it.

With right sides together and the edges aligned, pin one edge of the waistband to the skirt's waist, and join the two with a ¼" (6 mm) seam. Turn the other edge of the waistband under ¼" (6 mm) on the skirt waist's wrong side, and topstitch through all layers ⅛" (3 mm) from the folded edge.

Topstitch the ends and top of waistband ⅛" (3 mm) from the folded edge, starting at the short end, sewing across the top of the band, and ending at the other short end.

12. Add Ties

Cut two ties with the grain for the outside waist of the skirt that are 30" (76 cm) long by 1½" (4 cm) wide, and two ties for the inside waist that are 20" (50 cm) long by 1¼" (3 cm) wide. Place one unfolded, raw-edged 30"- (76-cm-) long tie at the end of the waistband on the right side of skirt's right front edge, with right sides together and matching the end of the tie to the end of the waistband. Stitch ¼" (6 mm) from the edge, wrap-stitching at the beginning and end of stitching line. Fold the tie back over the sewn edge, and stitch the edge again ¼" (6 mm) from the fold, wrap-stitching again at the beginning and end of the seam to produce a clean-finished edge that encases the seam allowances. Place the other 30" (76-cm) tie at the side seam, and stitch it in place the same way you attached the first tie.

Attach one of the 20" (50-cm) ties to the left front waistband and the other one inside the skirt at the waistband at the side seam, stitching them in place the same way as you attached the longer ties.

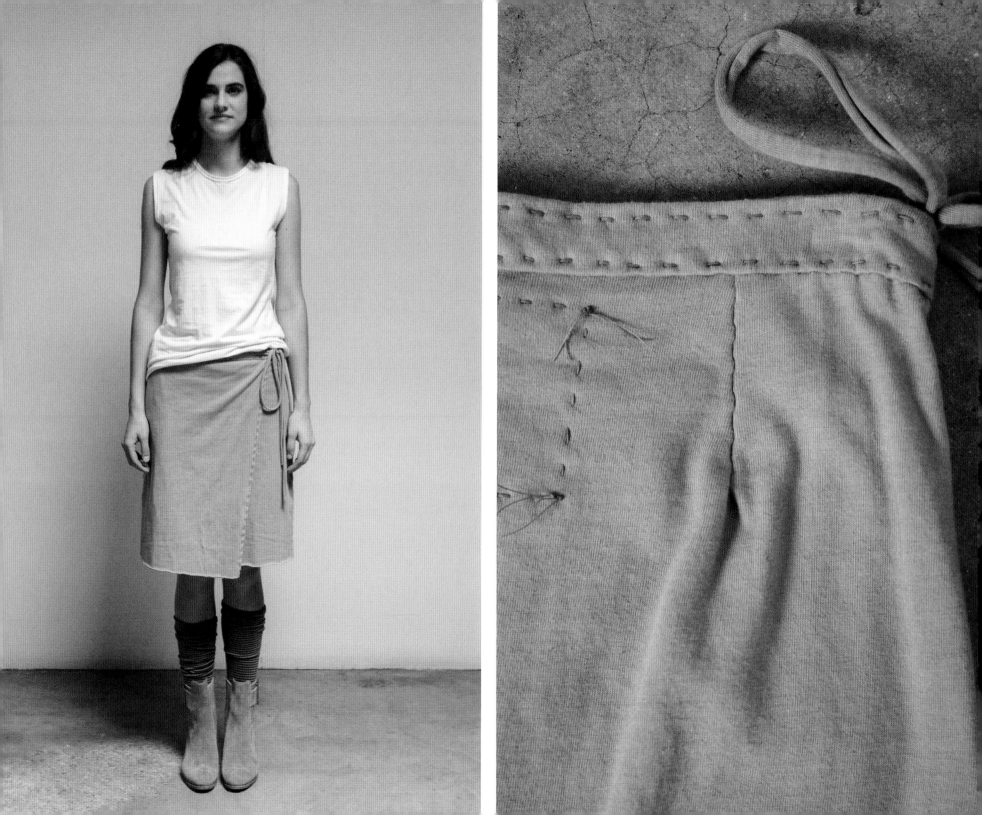

Alabama Studio Sewing + Design

The third book in our sewing series offers a wider range of garment patterns than the earlier two books, including tops, skirts, and dresses, and features more advanced and elaborate stitching techniques. We have come to call the garments in the third book our "classics."

This was our first book to include an index—like the one on page 164—that lists our design choices: garment style, fabric weight and color, thread color, and seaming, embroidery, stenciling, and beading choices. We thought we were creating this index to help readers, but I think it helps us in-house as much if not more. We use it for organization and inspiration, to refine how we run our Studio Style DIY department and, along with the two earlier books, to run the School of Making, the newer educational arm of our business.

Remember to review the construction and embellishment techniques in Part 3 (starting on page 126) before beginning a project.

Fitted Dress/Top/Tunic/Skirt Master Pattern

The master pattern for the Fitted Dress/Skirt on this book's CD can be used to make the Fitted Dress in all its seven variations—Short Fitted Dress, Long Fitted Dress, Fitted T-Shirt Top, Fitted Tunic, Short Skirt, Mid-Length Skirt, and Long Skirt.

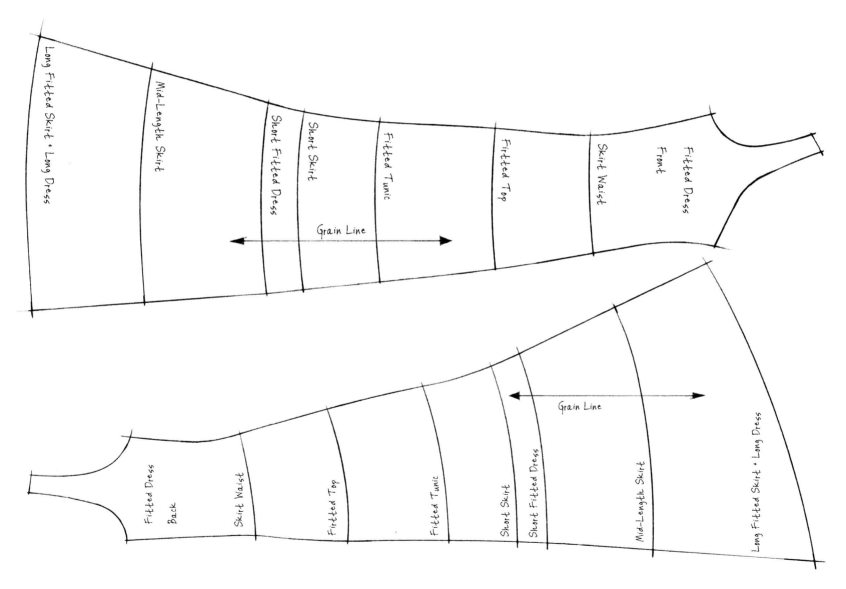

T-Shirt Top/Bolero Master Pattern

The master pattern for the T-Shirt Top on this book's CD includes the Bolero pattern. Both garments can be made sleeveless or with any of the four sleeve variations provided: long and fluted, ¾, short, and cap sleeves. See page 121 for more on sleeves.

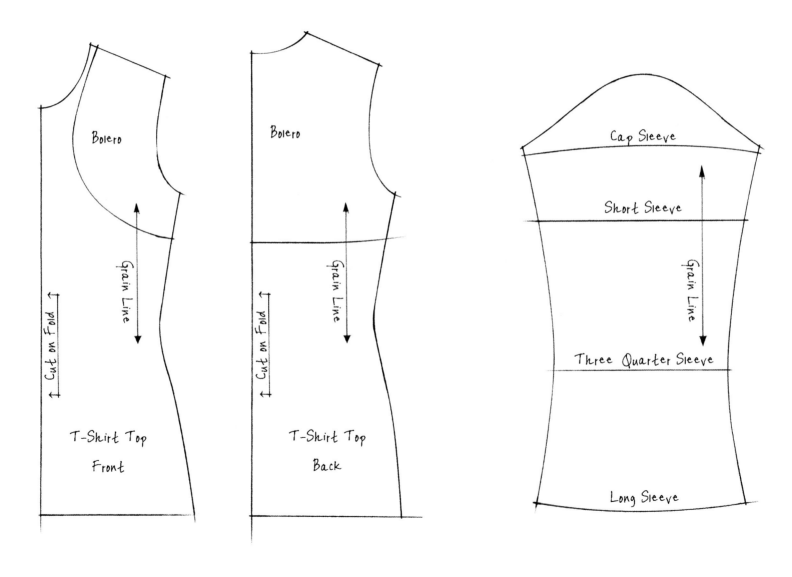

T-Shirt Top

This is our classic T-Shirt Top, which we also use for a sleeveless shell. The top has a slightly fitted waist and a longer length than a standard T-shirt. Over the years, we have offered this T-shirt with various sleeve styles, four of which are provided with the pattern: long and fluted, ¾, short, and cap. These sleeves can also be used with our new A-Line Dress on page 18. The top measures about 26" (66 cm) from the shoulder and can be shortened or lengthened easily by following the instructions on page 112 (see the chart on page 174 for yardage requirements).

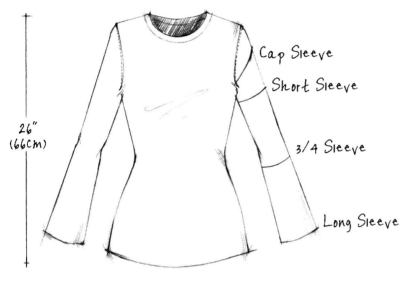

26"
(66cm)

Cap Sleeve

Short Sleeve

3/4 Sleeve

Long Sleeve

T-Shirt Top with sleeve variations

T-Shirt Top Instructions

SUPPLIES

Basic sewing supplies listed on page 128

T-Shirt Top pattern from this book's CD

60"- (1.5-m-) wide light- or medium-weight cotton-jersey fabric (see page 130) in one color, for top layer (see chart on page 174 for yardage needed)

60"- (1.5-m-) wide light- or medium-weight cotton-jersey fabric in a second color, for backing layer (optional)

1. Prepare and Cut Out Pattern

Print out the T-Shirt Top pattern from the CD (see page 86), and use paper scissors to cut the pattern to the desired size (see also "Mixing and Matching Pattern Sizes" on page 88), cutting as close as possible to the black cutting line. The T-Shirt Top pattern has two main pattern pieces and an optional sleeve in four styles, with a ¼" (6 mm) seam allowance built into all pattern edges.

2. Cut Top Pattern Pieces

Lay out your top-layer fabric flat, and then fold the fabric's width in half with the grain (see page 135), with wrong sides together and the edges aligned, creating two layers. Place the pattern front on top of the folded yardage, making sure the pattern and fabric grain lines run in the same direction (note that we prefer holding or weighting the pattern to pinning it on the fabric, which often skews the cotton jersey and makes the cutting uneven). With tailor's chalk, trace around the pattern's edges, remove the pattern, and use fabric scissors to cut out the traced pattern piece, cutting just inside the chalked line to remove it entirely. Repeat this step on the remaining yardage with the pattern's back. You will now have a total of two cut pieces for your T-Shirt. If you want sleeves, repeat this process with a double layer of fabric and the T-Shirt sleeve pattern of your choice to cut out two sleeves.

3. Baste Neckline and Armholes

To ensure that neckline and armholes do not stretch while you are constructing the T-Shirt, use a single strand of all-purpose thread to baste (see page 136) the neckline and armhole edges of each cut piece, as noted on the pattern pieces.

4. Add Stenciling and/or Embroidery (optional)

If you'd like to stencil your garment, add this to the right side only of the cut T-Shirt pieces, and let the stenciled images (see page 146) dry thoroughly before proceeding. Then embellish the pieces as desired. If you are adding beading, avoid beading in the ¼" (6 mm) seam allowance.

5. Prepare for Construction

After completing any embellishment, align and pin the front and back of the T-Shirt together at the shoulder, with right sides together. (Or, if you want to make the seams visible on the garment's right side, position the cut pieces with wrong sides together.)

6. Sew Shoulder Seams

Thread your needle, "love your thread," and knot off (see pages 132–133). Using a straight stitch (see page 136), sew the pinned pieces together at the shoulder, starting at the top edge of the T-Shirt's armhole and stitching ¼" (6 mm) from the fabric's cut edges across to the neckline. Begin and end the seam by wrap-stitching (see page 144) its edges to secure them.

7. Fell Shoulder Seams (optional)

Fell the seams by joining the seam allowances toward the back of your T-Shirt and topstitching the allowances ⅛" (3 mm) from the cut edges (down the center of the seam allowances), using a straight stitch and wrap-stitching the beginning and end of the seam.

8. Add Sleeves (optional)

Pin the cut sleeves to the T-Shirt armholes, matching the sleeve's front armhole edge with the front of the T-Shirt and the sleeve's back armhole edge with the back of the T-Shirt. Pin the pieces together securely, working in the excess fabric with pins. Thread your needle, "love your thread," and knot off. Using a straight stitch, sew the pinned pieces together at the armhole, wrap-stitching both ends of the seam. Either leave the seam floating or fold the seam allowances toward the sleeve and fell them down the center (see page 145).

9. Sew T-Shirt Body at Side Seams

Pin together the front, back, and optional sleeves at the side seams, with the edges aligned. Whether you are making a sleeveless garment or one with sleeves, join the side seams with a straight stitch, wrap-stitching them at the beginning and end. Start stitching at the bottom edge of the T-Shirt's hem, and sew the side and sleeve seams (for a garment with sleeves) in one continuous pass, which produces a better-fitting armhole than sewing the side seams and sleeves separately and then inserting the sleeves into the armholes. After stitching the side/sleeve seam, fold the seam allowances toward the back, and fell the seam.

10. Bind Neckline and Armholes (for sleeveless top)

Use a rotary cutter, cutting mat, and large plastic ruler to cut 1¼"- (3-cm-) wide strips of leftover fabric across the grain to use for binding the neckline and armholes. You will need a total of about 60" (1.5 m) of cut strips. Attaching the binding will be easier if you cut one continuous binding strip for the edge being bound—for example, cut one neckline binding strip long enough to go around the entire neckline.

Use an iron to press each cut binding strip in half lengthwise, with wrong sides together, being careful not to stretch the fabric as you press it. To bind the T-Shirt's neckline, start at the center-back neckline, encasing the neckline's raw edge inside the folded binding and pinning or basting the binding in place as you work (note that the binding strip's raw edges will show). If the binding strip is not long enough to cover the edge fully that you are binding, add a new binding strip as needed by overlapping the raw edges of the existing and new strips by ½" (12 mm). At the center-back point, similarly overlap the binding's raw edges by ½" (12 mm) to finish, trimming away the excess binding. Using the stretch stitch of your choice, sew through all layers and down the middle of the binding to permanently attach it. Repeat the process to finish each armhole on a sleeveless garment.

Then remove or simply break the neckline and armhole basting stitches by pulling gently on one end of the thread. If some basting stitches remain embedded in the binding, it is fine to leave them since, with the thread broken, the remaining stitches will not restrict the fabric's stretch.

Design Variation

T-SHIRT TOP WITH GODETS

This version of the T-Shirt Top has godets, or triangular panels, inserted in the front and back and in the side seams to add a bit more flare at the hips (which I always need). This godet pattern is included on the CD at the back of this book.

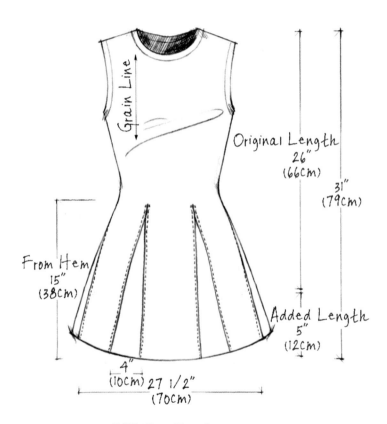

T-Shirt Top with godets

Basic sewing supplies listed on page 128

T-Shirt pattern printed from this book's CD

60"- (1.5-m-) wide light- or medium-weight cotton-jersey fabric (see page 130) for T-Shirt body and optional sleeves in one color (refer to chart on page 174 for yardage needed)

1. Prepare and Cut Pattern Pieces

Print out the T-Shirt Top pattern from the CD (see page 86) and use paper scissors to cut out the pattern to your desired size (see also "Mixing and Matching Pattern Sizes" on page 88), cutting as close as possible to the black cutting line.

2. Cut Pattern Pieces and Godets

Using fabric scissors, cut out your T-Shirt Top pattern pieces, adding 5" (12 cm) to the length of each piece. Fold the cut front panel's width in half along the fabric's length, and measure and mark 2½" (6 cm) from the bottom of the folded center line, using tailor's chalk. On each side of the center-front line, cut a slit 15" (38 cm) long in the panel. When the front is laid flat, your slits will be 4" (10 cm) apart. Repeat these steps on the T-Shirt's back panel.

Cut six godets, or triangular pieces, 4½" (11 cm) wide at the bottom by 16" (40.5 cm) long by ½" (12 mm) at the top, which you will sew into the slits and side seams of your T-Shirt.

3. Insert Godets

Carefully pin each godet into the slits and into your side seams, with right sides together, and sew together, using a ¼" (6 mm) seam allowance. You could also sew in the godets with the fabric wrong sides together for outside floating seams, as we did on the garment shown. This produces floating seams with seam allowances that will be visible on the garment's right side.

Thread your needle, "love your thread," and knot off (see pages 132–133), and seam the individual pieces together with a straight stitch, wrap-stitching the beginning and end of each seam (see page 144). Repeat this process with the back of the shirt. Note that we finished the top of each godet with a cross-stitch to secure the points and then trimmed away the excess fabric.

4. Construct T-Shirt Top

Construct your shirt with new panels, following instructions on page 46.

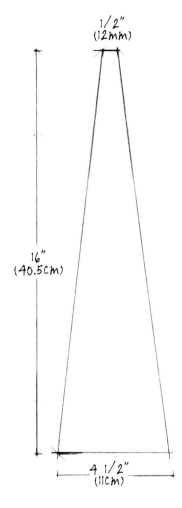

1/2"
(12mm)

16"
(40.5cm)

4 1/2"
(11cm)

Godet pattern

Design Variation

T-SHIRT TOP WITH PRINCESS SEAMS

Long rounded seams, commonly called princess seams, are a flattering way to add contour and shape at the bust and/or waistline of a garment. This added shaping is an integral feature of our Camisole Dress/Tank/Top on page 67 and the Corset on page 73.

Here we show you how to add princess seams to our T-Shirt Top by tracing the princess seams from the side-front pattern piece of the Camisole Dress onto the T-Shirt Top pattern. This adaptation can be used on virtually any garment pattern when a very feminine silhouette is desired.

When you are making this sort of advanced adaptation to a paper pattern, we recommend that you review our guidelines starting on page 90 and make an unembellished basic (see page 124) as a test. If it doesn't fit exactly as you like, then tweak to your liking before adding embellishments.

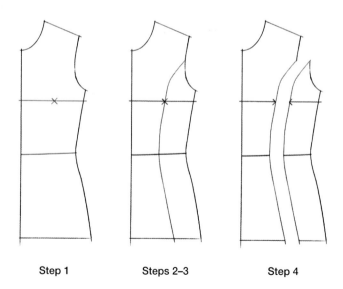

Step 1   Steps 2–3   Step 4

SUPPLIES

Basic patternmaking and sewing supplies listed on page 128

T-Shirt pattern printed from this book's CD

Camisole Dress pattern printed from this book's CD

60"- (1.5 m-) wide light- or medium-weight cotton-jersey fabric for T-Shirt body and sleeves in one color (refer to chart on page 174 for yardage needed)

1. Trace the T-Shirt Top pattern onto new pattern paper.

2. Lay the Camisole Dress side-front pattern piece over your T-shirt Front pattern piece, matching the bust lines and armholes.

3. Trace the princess seam onto your T-Shirt Top pattern on each side—right front and left front.

4. Cut the T-Shirt pattern apart at the princess seam.

5. Add a backing layer of pattern paper behind the cut-apart T-Shirt pattern, and add a ¼" (6 mm) seam allowance to each of the two cut edges making up each princess seam. This will be your finished paper pattern.

6. If desired, repeat this process for the T-Shirt Top back pattern.

7. Cut out your garment following instructions for the Camisole Dress on page 70. If desired, cut out sleeves from the T-Shirt Top pattern.

8. Add optional stenciling (see page 146) and/or embroidery (see page 138).

9. Follow the instructions on page 70 for constructing the Camisole Dress for your T-Shirt Top body, and the instructions on page 46 for adding the (optional) sleeves.

Design Variation

T-SHIRT WITH FRONT AND BACK STRIPE

This simple garment alteration can be used to increase the size of our T-Shirt Top (or any garment for that matter) but becomes a strong design element on its own. You can create the variation easily by not placing your T-Shirt Top pattern on the fold (as you are instructed to do for our basic T-Shirt) but instead by following the cutting instructions at right. This cutting variation produces a center seam on the front and back in which you can insert a stripe of fabric. The width of the center-front stripe can vary from a ¼" (6 mm) sliver to a 2" (5 cm) stripe, as shown here. Use a similarly colored cotton jersey for a subtle, elegant effect or bright contrasting colors for a bold statement.

We used floating seams (see page 144) when sewing in the stripe. The floating seams extend right up through the ribbing at the neckline. To produce this design detail, before sewing the stripe in the front and back panels, sew ribbing to the neck edge of each of the panels and stripes. Then construct the top, sewing through the seam and the ribbing as one piece. Further define your piece by using an embroidery stitch to sew the front stripe into place (see page 138), or stenciling (see page 146), or adding appliqué (see page 151) to your center-front and/or -back stripes.

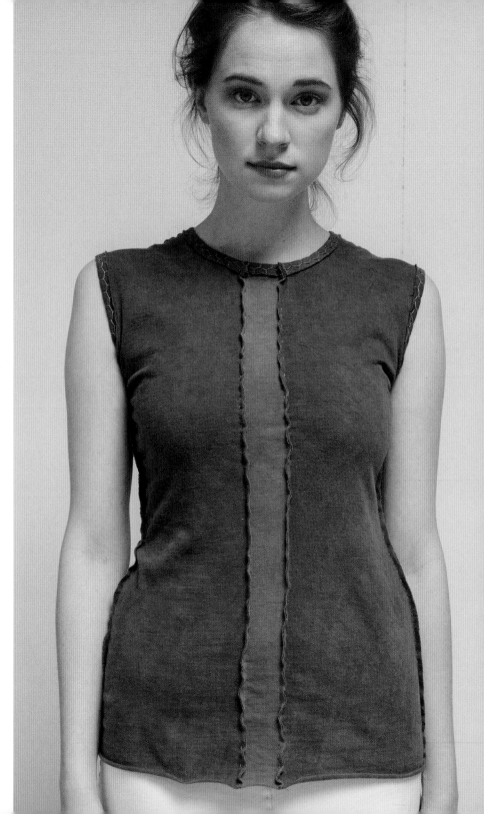

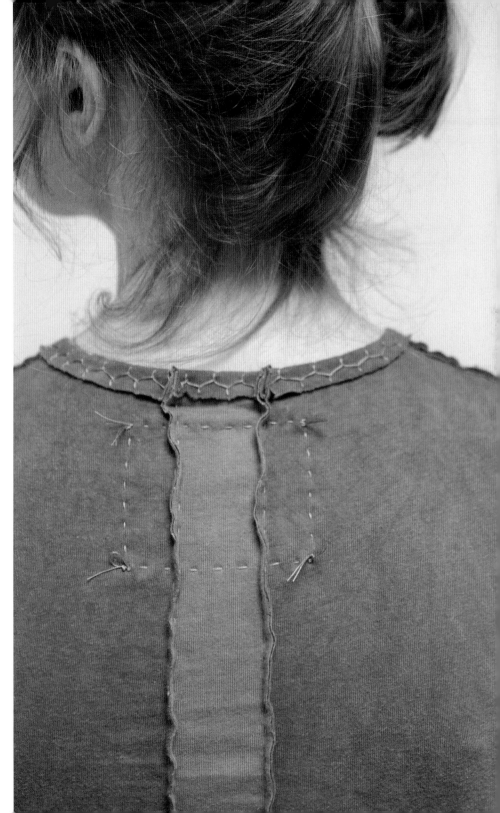

SUPPLIES

Basic sewing supplies listed on page 128

T-Shirt pattern printed from this book's CD

60"- (1.5-m-) wide light- or medium-weight cotton-jersey fabric
(see page 130) for T-Shirt body and optional sleeves in one color
(refer to chart on page 174 for yardage needed)

2 pieces of cotton jersey, at least 2" (5 cm) wide and
length of shirt (in same weight jersey as body)

1. Prepare and Cut Pattern Pieces

Print out the T-Shirt Top pattern from the CD (see page 86) and use paper scissors to cut out the pattern to your desired size (see also "Mixing and Matching
Pattern Sizes" on page 88), cutting as close as possible to the black cutting line.

2. Cut Out Pattern and Stripes

Cut your T-Shirt pattern pieces from cotton jersey, following instructions for
T-Shirt Top on page 46. Working with the two small pieces of cotton jersey
and using your rotary cutter, cutting mat, and ruler, cut two 2"- (5-cm-) wide
stripes, one the length of front panel and the other the length of the back panel.

3. Cut Front and Back Panels in Half

Fold the cut front panel's width in half along the fabric's length, with wrong sides
together and the edges aligned, creating two layers, and cut the panel in half
along the fold. Repeat with the back panel. Note that you could also produce
the half-panels for the front and back of your T-shirt by cutting both pattern
pieces on two layers of fabric but NOT placing the pattern pieces on the fold,
as called for on the pattern pieces and the garment instructions.

4. Insert Stripes and Construct T-Shirt Top

Pin the two sides of the shirt's front panels to the 2" (5 cm) stripe, with wrong
sides together, the edges aligned, and leaving a ¼" (6 mm) seam allowance
on each edge, which will give your finished shirt a 1½" (4 cm) stripe down
the center. Thread your needle, "love your thread," and knot off (see pages
132–133); join the half-panels and stripes with floating seams (see page 144),
wrap-stitching the beginning and end of each seam to secure it. Repeat this
process with shirt's back panels. Construct shirt with the new, modified panels,
following instructions for T-Shirt Top. (To bind the T-Shirt neck using floating
seams, see the construction notes in second paragraph on facing page.)

Bolero

The Bolero has long been one of our favorite cover-ups at Alabama Chanin, now joined by the Classic Cardigan on page 30. The Bolero works well with any of our sleeveless tops and dresses. Many women who are uncomfortable showing their arms in sleeveless garments gravitate to this piece for coverage. The Bolero can be made in four different sleeve variations or sleeveless. The instructions below can be used for either a single- or double-layer garment. The Bolero measures about 11" (28 cm) from the center back to the bottom back edge. (See the chart on page 174 for yardage needed for this garment.)

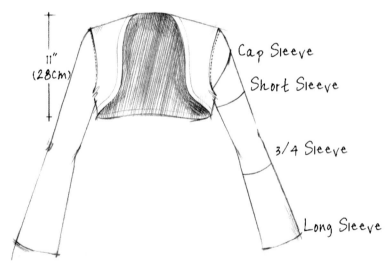

Cap Sleeve

Short Sleeve

3/4 Sleeve

Long Sleeve

11" (28cm)

Bolero with sleeve variations

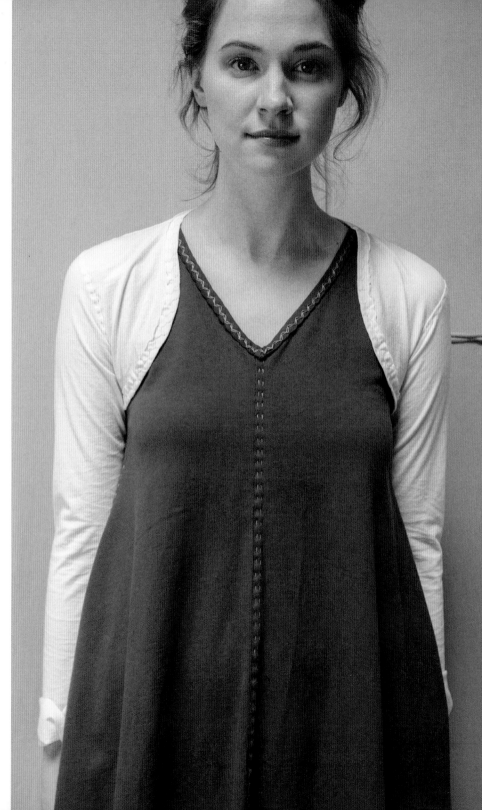

Bolero Instructions

SUPPLIES

Basic sewing supplies listed on page 128

Bolero pattern printed from this book's CD

60"- (1.5-m-) wide light- or medium-weight cotton-jersey fabric (see page 130) in one color, for top layer (see chart on page 174 for yardage needed)

60"- (1.5-m-) wide light- or medium-weight cotton-jersey fabric in a second color, for backing layer (optional)

1. Prepare and Cut Pattern Pieces

Print out the Bolero pattern from the CD (see page 86), and use paper scissors to cut it to your desired size (see also "Mixing and Matching Pattern Sizes" on page 88), cutting as close as possible to the black cutting line. The Bolero pattern has two main pattern pieces and an optional sleeve in four styles (see page 121 for all sleeve options), with a ¼" (6 mm) seam allowance built into all pattern edges.

2. Cut Top-Layer Pattern Pieces

Lay out your top-layer fabric flat, and then fold the fabric's width in half with the grain (see page 135), with wrong sides together and the edges aligned, creating two layers. Place the Bolero pattern front on top of the folded yardage, making sure the pattern and fabric grain lines run in the same direction (we prefer holding or weighting the pattern instead of pinning it on the fabric, which often skews the cotton jersey and makes the cutting uneven). Use tailor's chalk to trace around the pattern's edges, remove the pattern, and use fabric scissors to cut out the traced pattern, cutting just inside the chalked line to remove it entirely. You will now have your two front pieces. Repeat this step on the remaining yardage with your Bolero pattern back, placing it on the fold, which will give you one back piece, or a total of three pieces for the garment's top layer. If you want to add sleeves to your Bolero, cut out the desired sleeve pattern from the remaining double-layered fabric to get two sleeves. Refer to page 121 for more on sleeves.

3. Cut Backing-Layer Pattern Pieces (for double-layer garment, optional)

If you want to make a double-layer garment, lay out your backing-layer fabric flat, and then fold the fabric's width in half along the fabric's length, with wrong sides together and the edges aligned, creating two layers. Then repeat the process in Step 2, using your cut front and back top-layer pieces as cutting guides, to cut three backing-layer pieces for the Bolero body. If you are adding sleeves to your Bolero, cut two backing-layer sleeves from the remaining double-layer fabric. You will now have a total of five backing-layer pieces, or ten pieces total for your garment.

4. Baste Bolero Body and Armholes

To ensure that the Bolero's curved shape and armholes on your cut fabric pieces do not stretch while you are constructing the garment, use a single strand of all-purpose thread to baste (see page 136) around the neckline, body, and armhole edges of each cut piece, as noted on the pattern piece.

5. Add Stenciling (optional)

If you'd like to stencil your garment, refer to the overview on page 146. Add the desired stenciling on the right side of only the Bolero's top layer, and let the image dry thoroughly.

6. Pin Pattern's Top and Backing Layers (for double-layer garment, optional)

Align each cut top-layer piece on the corresponding backing-layer piece, with both fabrics facing right side up, and pat the layers into place with your fingertips so that their edges match. Securely pin together the two layers of each piece, being sure to scatter your pins across the face of the project piece (see page 39).

7. Add Embellishment (optional)

Complete all the embellishments (see pages 132–159) that you want to add to your project. If you are adding beading, be sure to avoid beading in the ¼" (6 mm) seam allowance.

8. Prepare for Construction

After completing any embellishment, choose how you want to work your seams from the list of options on pages 144–145. Begin constructing the Bolero by pinning the front and back panels together at the shoulder with the edges aligned.

9. Sew Shoulder Seams

Thread your needle, "love your thread," and knot off (see pages 132–133). Using a straight stitch (see page 136), sew the pinned pieces together at the shoulder, starting at the top edge of the Bolero's armhole and stitching ¼" (6 mm) from the fabric's cut edges across to the neckline. Begin and end the seam by wrap-stitching (see page 144) its edges to secure them. Fell your seam by folding over the seam allowances towards the back of your Bolero and topstitching the seam allowances ⅛" (3 mm) from the cut edges (down the center of the seam allowances), using a straight stitch and wrap-stitching both ends of the seam.

10. Add Sleeves (optional)

Pin the cut sleeves to the Bolero's armholes, matching each sleeve's front armhole edge to the Bolero's front armhole edge and the sleeve's back edge to the Bolero's back armhole edge. Pin the edges securely, working in the excess fabric with the pins. Thread your needle, "love your thread," and knot off. Using a straight stitch, sew the pinned pieces together at the armhole, wrap-stitching both ends of seam. Either leave the seams floating, or fold the seam allowances toward the sleeve and fell them down the center (see page 145).

11. Sew Side Seams

Pin together the front, back, and optional sleeves at the side seams. Whether you are making a sleeveless garment or one with sleeves, join the side seams with a straight stitch, and wrap-stitch both ends of the seams. Start stitching at the bottom edge of the Bolero's hem, and sew the side and optional sleeve seams in one continuous pass, which produces a better-fitting armhole than sewing the side seams and sleeves separately and then inserting the sleeves into armholes. After stitching the side/sleeve seam, fold the seam allowances toward the back, and fell the seam.

12. Bind Neckline and Armholes (for sleeveless bolero)

Use a rotary cutter, cutting mat, and large plastic ruler to cut 1¼"- (4-cm-) wide strips of leftover fabric across the grain to use for binding the neckline and armholes. You will need a total of about 60" (1.5 m) of cut strips. Note that attaching the binding will be easier if you cut the binding for a particular area long enough to fit that entire area so that you do not have to piece the binding—for example, cut one piece of neckline binding that is long enough to go entirely around the whole neckline.

Use an iron to press each cut binding strip in half lengthwise, with wrong sides together, being careful not to stretch the fabric as you press it. Starting at the Bolero's center-back neckline, encase the neckline's raw edge (the neckline, front edges, and bottom edge) inside the folded binding, pinning or basting the binding in place as you work (note that the binding strip's raw edges will show on the garment's right side). If the binding strip is not long enough to fully cover the edge you are binding, add a new binding strip by overlapping the existing and new strips' raw edges by ½" (12 mm). At the center-back point, similarly overlap the binding's raw edges by ½" (12 mm) to finish, trimming away any excess binding.

Using the stretch stitch of your choice (see page 138) to sew the binding permanently in place, stitch through all layers and down the middle of the binding. Repeat the process to finish each armhole if you have chosen to make a sleeveless garment. Remove or simply break the neckline and armhole basting stitches by pulling gently on one end of the thread. If some basting stitches remain embedded in the binding, it is fine to leave them in place since the thread is broken, and the remaining stitches will not restrict the fabric's stretch.

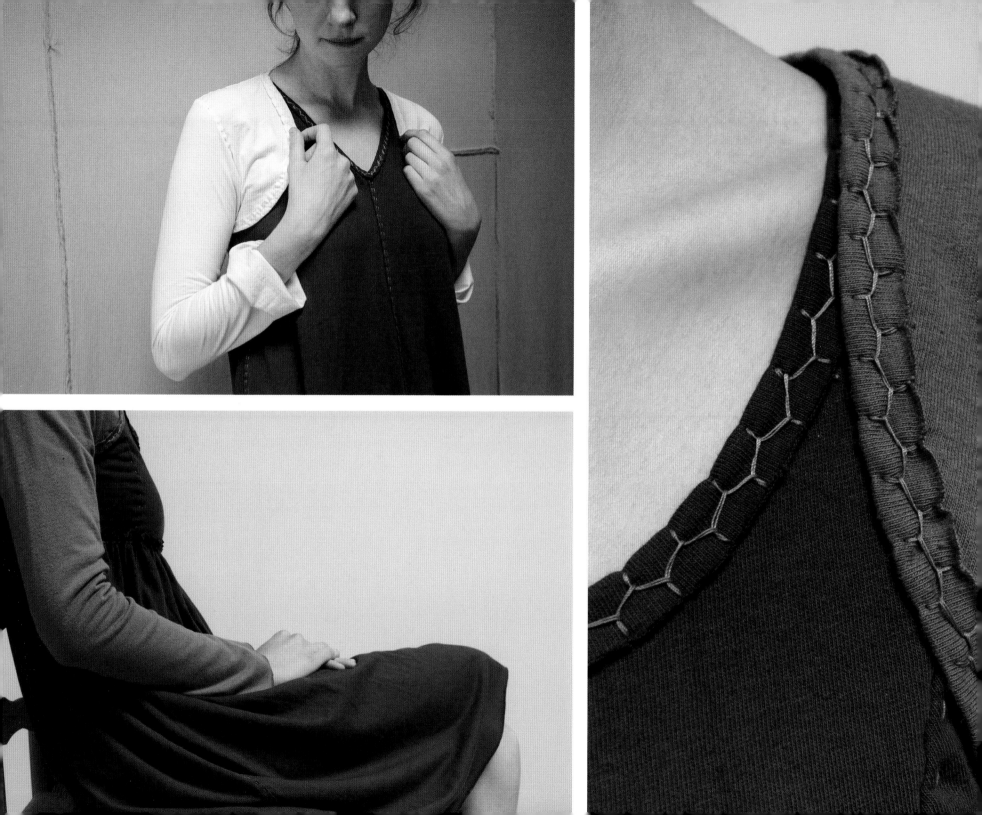

Fitted Top/Tunic/Dress

All of these pieces can be made following the instructions for the A-Line Dress on page 18. The only difference happens in Step 10, when you bind the neckline. At that point, for these pieces, you need to cut 80" (2 m) of 1¼-" (4-cm-) wide binding instead of the shorter amount required for the A-Line Dress. Then, starting at the dress's center-back neckline, encase the neckline's raw edge inside the folded binding, pinning or basting the binding in place as you work (note that the binding strip's raw edges will show). Add a new binding strip, as needed, by overlapping the existing and new strips' short raw edges by ½" (12 mm); when you reach the center-back point again, overlap the binding's short raw edges by about ½" (12 mm) to finish the binding, trimming away any excess binding. Using the stretch stitch of your choice (see page 138) to sew the binding in place permanently, stitch through all layers and down the middle of the binding.

Repeat the process above to bind and finish each armhole. Remove or simply break the neckline and armhole basting stitches by pulling gently on one end of the thread. If some basting stitches remain embedded in the binding, it is fine to leave them in place since the thread is broken, and the remaining stitches will not restrict the fabric's stretch.

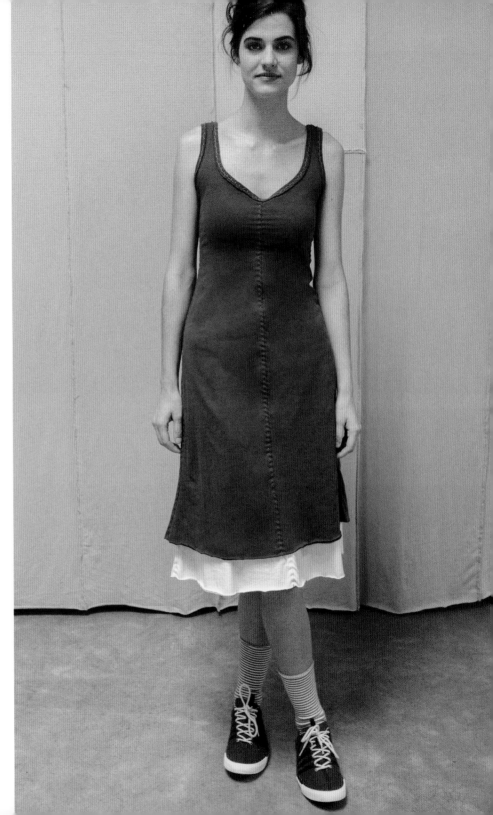

FITTED TOP

This top has thin straps, a scooped neckline, and a shaped center-front seam to give lift in the bust. It is fitted at the waist and flares slightly from the high hip. The top measures about 24" (61 cm) from the shoulder to the hem.

FITTED TUNIC

This tunic has thin straps, a scooped neckline, and a shaped center-front seam to give lift in the bust. It is fitted at the waist and flares slightly at the high hip. The tunic measures about 30½" (84 cm) from the shoulder to the hem.

SHORT FITTED DRESS

This dress has thin straps, a scooped neckline, and a shaped center-front seam to give lift in the bust. It is fitted at the waist and flares slightly at the high hip. The dress measures about 40" (1 m) from the shoulder to the hem.

LONG FITTED DRESS

This long version of our Fitted Dress is an Alabama Chanin favorite. It is flattering and comfortable, with a clean silhouette and a small train, which can be elaborately embroidered for special occasions. The dress measures about 55" (1.4 m) from the shoulder to the front hem and 61" (1.5 m) from the shoulder to the back-train hem.

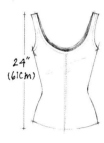
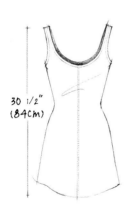
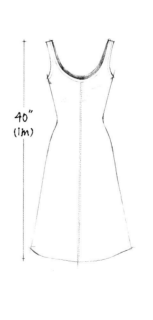
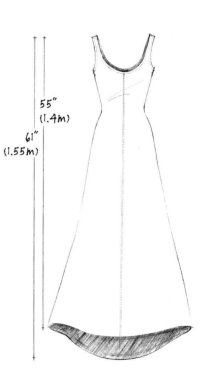

All of these pieces can be shortened or lengthened easily at the bottom edge by making a perimeter alteration (see page 112) or at the waistline by making an internal alteration (see page 114).

Short/Mid-Length/Long Fitted Skirt

The Long Fitted Dress pattern includes the three skirt variations shown on the facing page. The directions on page 62 apply to the Short, Mid-Length, and Long Skirt. Only the fabric yardage needed for each skirt is different (see the yardage chart on page 174). This four-panel skirt has a more streamlined silhouette than the six-panel Gore Skirt (see page 67) and the four panel A-Line Swing Skirt (see page 76). The master pattern for this skirt is shown with the Fitted Dress master pattern on page 43.

SHORT FITTED SKIRT

This simple, pull-on Short Skirt is great for just about every occasion, and its small cut pattern pieces are perfect for elaborate embroidery. The skirt measures about 21" (53 cm) from the waist to the bottom edge. Our Short Skirt is more fitted than our A-line Swing Skirt (see page 76), offering a cleaner silhouette with a slight flare to the hem.

MID-LENGTH FITTED SKIRT

Like the Short Skirt, this pull-on Mid-Length Skirt is extremely versatile, and its small cut pattern pieces are ideal for intricate embroidery. The skirt measures about 32" (81 cm) from the waist to the bottom edge.

LONG FITTED SKIRT

This Long Skirt with a small train has become a staple in nearly every Alabama Chanin collection. Depending on how it is embellished and accessorized, it can be worn as everything from eveningwear to a beach cover-up. The train on the back of the skirt is 4" (10 cm) longer than the front hem. The skirt measures approximately 40½" (1 m) from the waist to the front hem and 44½" (1.1 m) from the waist to the back-train hem.

21"
(53m)

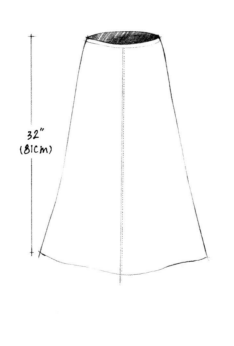

32"
(81Cm)

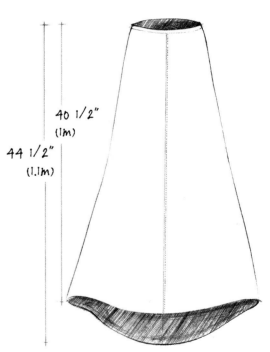

40 1/2"
(1m)

44 1/2"
(1.1m)

All of these pieces can be shortened or lengthened easily at the bottom edge by making a perimeter alteration (see page 112).

Fitted Skirt Instructions

SUPPLIES

Basic sewing supplies listed on page 128

Fitted Skirt pattern printed from this book's CD

60"- (1.5-m-) wide light- or medium-weight cotton-jersey fabric (see page 130) in one color, for top layer (see chart on page 174 for yardage needed)

60"- (1.5-m-) wide cotton-jersey fabric in a second color, for backing layer (optional)

1 yard (.9 m) of 1"- (2.5-cm-) wide fold-over elastic

1. Prepare and Cut Pattern

Print out the Skirt pattern from the CD (see page 86), and use paper scissors to cut the pattern to your desired size (also see "Mixing and Matching Pattern Sizes" on page 88), cutting as close as possible to the black cutting line. The pattern has two pieces—a front panel and a back panel—with a ¼" (6 mm) seam allowance built into all the pattern edges.

2. Cut Top-Layer Pattern Pieces

Lay out your top-layer fabric flat, and then fold the fabric's width in half with the grain (see page 135), with wrong sides together and the edges aligned, creating two layers. Position the front pattern on top of the folded yardage, making sure the pattern and fabric grain lines run in the same direction (note that we prefer holding or weighting the pattern to pinning it on the fabric, which often skews the cotton jersey and makes the cutting uneven). With tailor's chalk, trace around the pattern's edges, remove the pattern, and use fabric scissors to cut out the traced pattern, cutting just inside the chalked line to remove it entirely. Repeat this step on the remaining top-layer fabric to cut four top layers for your skirt.

3. Cut Backing-Layer Pattern Pieces (for double-layer garment, optional)

If you want to make a double-layer garment, lay out the backing-layer fabric flat, and then fold the fabric's width in half with the grain, with wrong sides together and the edges aligned, creating two layers. Then repeat the process in Step 2 to cut four backing-layer pieces, for a total of eight pieces for the garment.

4. Baste Waistline

To ensure that the waistline on your cut fabric pieces does not stretch while you construct your skirt, use a single strand of all-purpose thread to baste (see page 136) each piece's waistline edge, as noted on the pattern.

5. Add Stenciling (optional)

If you'd like to stencil your garment, refer to page 146. Add the stenciling on the right side only of the skirt's top layer, and let the image dry thoroughly.

6. Pin Pattern's Top and Backing Layers (for double-layer garment, optional)

Repeat Step 6 of the A-Line Dress instructions (see page 19).

7. Add Embellishment (optional)

Repeat Step 7 of the A-Line Dress instructions (see page 19).

8. Prepare for Construction

After completing any embellishment, choose how you want to work your seams from the list of options on pages 144–145. Begin constructing your skirt by aligning and pinning each pair of adjacent panels.

9. Construct Skirt

Thread your needle, "love your thread," and knot off (see pages 132–133). Using a straight stitch (see page 136), sew the pinned pieces together, starting at the top edge of the skirt's waistline and stitching ¼" (6 mm) from the fabric's cut edges down to the bottom edge. Be sure to begin and end the seam by wrap-stitching (see page 144) its edges. Fell your seams by folding over each seam's allowances ⅛" (3 mm) from the cut edges and stitching down the center of the seam allowances, using a straight stitch and wrap-stitching the beginning and end of the seam to secure it. Repeat this process for the skirt's side seams.

10. Bind Waistline

Using ⅞"- (2-cm-) wide fold-over elastic and starting at the skirt's center-back waistline, encase the waistline's raw edge with the folded elastic, pinning or basting it in place as you work. Overlap the elastic's raw edges at the center back by about ½" (12 mm), and trim off any excess elastic. Using the stretch stitch of your choice (see page 138) to sew the elastic in place permanently, stitch through all the layers down the middle of the elastic.

ADDING PATCH POCKETS

You will find a pattern piece for a five-side patch pocket with the Fitted Skirt pattern and a rectangular patch pocket with the Classic Coat pattern on this book's CD. Either style can be used for any project in this book. You can cut this pocket single- or double-layer, as desired for your individual project. When working with double-layered pockets, simply treat the two layers as one. We recommend completing the entire garment and then figuring out where you want to place the pockets by trying the garment on. To construct each pocket, first fold down the pocket's top edge 1" (2.5 cm) to the wrong side on the fold line, and steam the fold with an iron.

Sew this folded top edge in place ¾" (2 cm) from the top edge, using a straight stitch and leaving the remaining edges raw. Repeat these initial steps for the second pocket, and pin the finished pair of pockets on the garment, making sure that they are evenly placed in relation to the center front and hem. Then stitch them into place with your stitch of choice, wrap-stitching the beginning and end at the pocket top.

We used a straight stitch for our version. For an added variation, you may want to add an embroidered binding around the outside edge of your pocket. You could also choose to cut a smaller version of this pocket, and stitch it to the inside of your garment for an inner pocket. In this case, stitch your inside pocket before adding your outside pocket.

Pocket top folded down and stitched

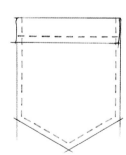

Pocket with sides and hem sewn to base fabric

Poncho

This versatile cover-up is just a strategically sewn rectangle of fabric. An Alabama Chanin favorite, it looks beautiful in every color and fabric style. Ponchos cut across the grain (see page 135) stretch out of shape over time, particularly around the neckline (since fabric cut on the cross-grain stretches more and has less "memory" than fabric cut with the grain). In our studio, to counter this tendency, we always cut two ponchos at once by folding the fabric in half along the grain line to create a double layer and then cutting through both layers, making one for ourselves and one to gift to a friend.

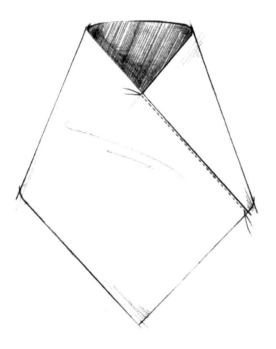

Poncho Instructions

SUPPLIES

Basic sewing supplies listed on page 128

Poncho pattern printed from this book's CD or one 24 x 54" (61 cm x 1.4 m) piece of pattern paper

60"- (1.5-m-) wide light- or medium-weight cotton-jersey fabric (see page 130) in one color, for top layer (see chart on page 174 for yardage needed)

60"- (1.5-m-) wide light- or medium-weight cotton-jersey fabric in a second color, for backing layer (optional)

1. Prepare and Cut Pattern

Print out the Poncho pattern from the CD (see page 86), and use paper scissors to cut it out, cutting as close as possible to the black cutting line. Alternatively, cut out a 24 x 54" (61 cm x 1.4 m) piece of pattern paper according to the specifications in the illustration below.

2. Cut Out Poncho

Lay out your fabric either single-layer (if you want to cut one poncho) or double-layer (if you want to cut two), folding the fabric's width for a double-layer poncho in half lengthwise along the grain, with wrong sides together and the edges aligned. Place the Poncho pattern on top of the fabric, making sure that the pattern and fabric grain lines run in the same direction (we prefer holding or weighting the pattern to pinning it on the fabric, which often skews the cotton

jersey and makes the cutting uneven). With tailor's chalk, trace around the pattern's edges, remove the pattern, and use fabric scissors to cut out the traced pattern, cutting just inside the chalked line to remove it entirely.

3. Add Stenciling and Embellishment (optional)

If you want to embellish your poncho, cut any additional fabric layers called for by your chosen embellishment, stencil the top fabric layer only (see page 146), and let the stenciling dry completely. Then align and pin the top and any backing layers, and complete all embellishments that you want to add, stitching through all fabric layers you are working with. If you are adding beading to your project, avoid beading in the ¼" (6 mm) seam allowance.

4. Pin and Assemble Poncho

Lay out your cut single-layer or multi-layer embroidered poncho pieces on a table, right side down. Bring the fabric's bottom right corner (A) up to meet the top left corner (C), and pin the rectangle's A-B edge to the C-D edge, starting at C and following the illustration. Thread your needle, "love your thread," and knot off (see pages 132–133). Using a straight stitch, sew the pinned pieces together, starting at point A/C, stitching ¼" (6 mm) from the fabric's cut edges, and ending at point B/D. Be sure to begin and end the seam by wrap-stitching its edges to secure them (see page 144). Leave the seam allowances floating.

5. Wash and Wear

We recommend washing the poncho before wearing it so that its raw edges will curl.

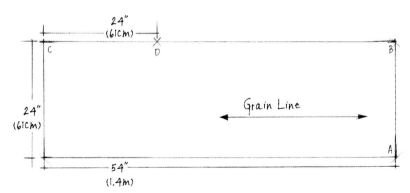

Poncho pattern

Alabama Studio Style

Our second book, *Alabama Studio Style*, is really about lifestyle. In addition to garments, it includes projects for the home as well as favorite recipes. The subtitle, *More Projects, Recipes, and Stories Celebrating Sustainable Fashion + Living*, really describes it well.

The basis of the garments in this book is one master pattern for the Camisole Dress, which can be worked in variations to complete seven garments: the Camisole and Tank Top, the Camisole and Tank Tunic, the Camisole and Tank Dress, and the Gore Skirt.

All of the garments shown on pages 66–71 are made from the master pattern on the facing page. All of these pieces except for the skirt can be made following the instructions for the Camisole/Tank Dress on page 70. To make the Gore Skirt, follow the instructions for the Fitted Skirt on page 62.

Be sure to review our basic construction and embellishment techniques in Part 3 (starting on page 126) before you begin a project.

Camisole and Tank Top/Tunic/Dress/Gore Skirt Master Patterns

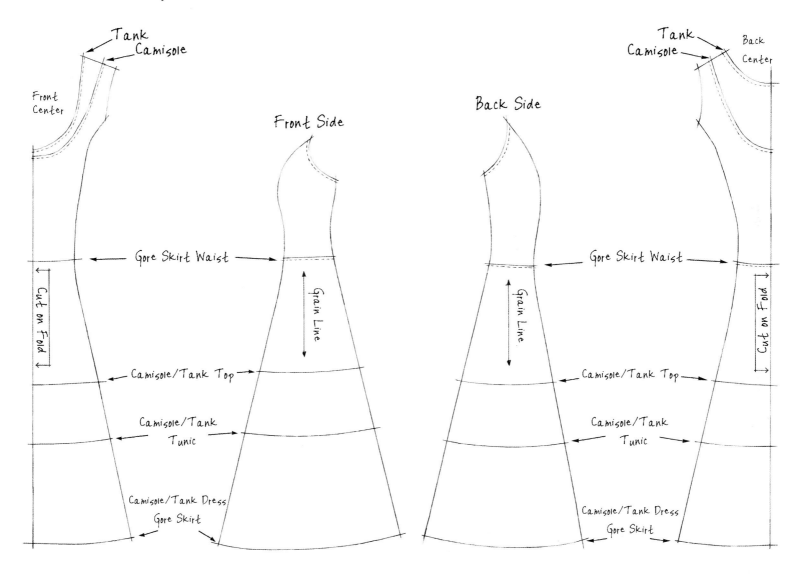

Tank

Camisole

Front Center

Front Side

Gore Skirt Waist

Cut on Fold

Grain Line

Camisole/Tank Top

Camisole/Tank Tunic

Camisole/Tank Dress

Gore Skirt

Back Side

Tank

Camisole

Back Center

Gore Skirt Waist

Grain Line

Cut on Fold

Camisole/Tank Top

Camisole/Tank Tunic

Camisole/Tank Dress

Gore Skirt

CAMISOLE AND TANK TOPS

The Camisole Top has thin straps, a revealing neckline, and a scooped-out back. The Tank Top has a higher back neckline and wider straps (indicated in red). Both tops are nipped in at the waist and at the curve of the back to flatter the figure. The fitted bust and waist provide support, and the top flares slightly from the waist. The top measures approximately 25" (63.5 cm) from the shoulder.

CAMISOLE AND TANK TUNICS

The Camisole Tunic has thin straps, a revealing neckline, and a scooped-out back. The Tank Top has a higher back neckline and wider straps (indicated in red). Both tops are nipped in at the waist and at the curve of the back to flatter the figure. The fitted bust and waist provide support, and the six-gore peplum of the tunic flares from the waist to accommodate most hip sizes. The tunic measures approximately 31" (79 cm) from the shoulder.

CAMISOLE AND TANK DRESSES

The Camisole Dress has thin straps, a revealing neckline, and a scooped-out back. The Tank Top has a higher back neckline and wider straps (indicated in red). Both tops are nipped in at the waist and at the curve of the back to flatter the figure. The fitted bust and waist provide support, and the six-gore skirt of the dress flares from the waist to accommodate most hip sizes. This dress measures approximately 40½" (1 m) from the shoulder.

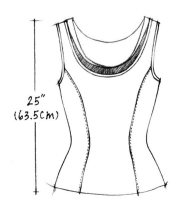

25"
(63.5Cm)

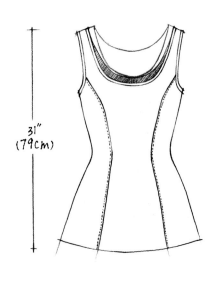

31"
(79Cm)

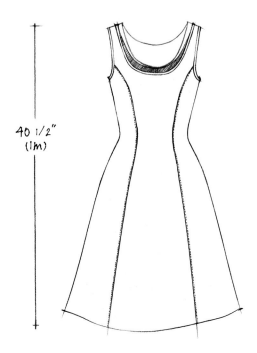

40 1/2"
(1m)

The red lines in each of the illustrations above show the higher back neck and wider strap lines for the Tank Top, Tank Tunic, and Tank Dress, which are otherwise the same as the Camisole Top, Tunic, and Dress.

GORE SKIRT

This six-gore, flared, pull-on skirt sits low on the waist and flares from the waist to accommodate most hip sizes. The flare of this Gore Skirt makes a much fuller shape and more playful silhouette than our A-Line Swing Skirt on page 76 and the straight and streamlined Fitted Skirt on page 60. The Gore Skirt measures 24" (61 cm) from the waist and has the simple fold-over elastic waistband (see page 129) that is so popular on all of our Alabama Chanin skirts.

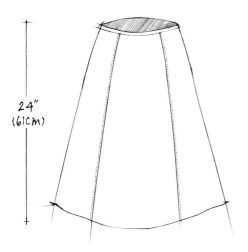

24"
(61cm)

Camisole/Tank Dress Instructions

SUPPLIES

Basic sewing supplies listed on page 128

Camisole/Tank Dress pattern printed from this book's CD

60"- (1.5-m-) wide light- or medium-weight cotton-jersey fabric (see page 130) in one color, for top layer (see chart on page 174 for yardage needed)

60"- (1.5-m-) wide light- or medium-weight cotton-jersey fabric in a second color, for backing layer (optional)

The instructions below are specifically for the Camisole Dress (either single- or double-layer); however, they can also be applied to the Tank Dress from page 70 and/or the Corset pattern from page 74.

1. Prepare and Cut Pattern

Print out the Camisole Dress pattern from the CD (see page 86), and use paper scissors to cut the printed pattern to your desired size (see also "Mixing and Matching Pattern Pieces" on page 88), cutting as close as possible to the black cutting line. The pattern has four pieces—a center front panel, a side front panel, a center back panel, and a side back panel—with a ¼" (6 mm) seam allowance built into all the pattern edges.

2. Cut Top-Layer Pattern Pieces

Lay out your top-layer fabric flat, and then fold the fabric's width in half with the grain (see page 135), with wrong sides together and the edges aligned, creating two layers. Place the Camisole Dress pattern front on top of the folded yardage, making sure the pattern and fabric grain lines (see page 135) run in the same direction and that the center front and center back pieces are on the fold. Use tailor's chalk to trace around the pattern's edges, remove the pattern, and cut out the traced pattern with fabric scissors, cutting just inside the chalked line to remove it entirely. (Note that we prefer holding or weighting the pattern to pinning it on the fabric, which, in the case of cotton jersey, often skews the fabric and makes the cutting uneven.) You will now have three front pieces. Repeat this step on the remaining yardage with your Camisole Dress back, which will give you three back pieces, for a total of six pieces for the garment's top layer.

3. Cut Backing-Layer Pattern Pieces (optional)

If you want to make a double-layer garment, lay out the backing fabric flat, and fold it in half as you did with the top-layer fabric, with wrong sides together and the edges aligned, to create two layers. Then repeat Step 2, using your cut front and back top-layer pieces as pattern guides, and cut a set of backing-layer pieces. You will now have six front pieces and six back dress pieces, for a total of twelve pieces.

4. Baste Neckline and Armholes

To ensure that the neckline and armholes on your cut fabric pieces do not stretch while you are constructing the dress, use a single strand of all-purpose thread to baste (see page 136) the neckline and armhole edges of each cut piece, as noted on the pattern pieces.

5. Add Stenciling (optional)

If you'd like to stencil your garment, refer to *Alabama Stitch Book*, *Alabama Studio Style*, *Alabama Studio Sewing + Design*, or the overview on page 146 of this book for stenciling and embellishment ideas and instructions. Add the stenciling as desired on the right side of the Camisole Dress's top layer only, and let the image dry thoroughly.

6. Pin Pattern's Top and Backing Layers (optional)

If you want to make a double-layer garment, align each cut top-layer piece on the corresponding backing-layer piece, with both fabrics facing right side up, and pat the layers into place with your fingertips so that their edges match. Securely pin together the two layers of each piece, being sure to scatter your pins across the face of the project piece, as shown on page 39.

7. Add Embellishment (optional)

Complete all the embellishments that you want to add to your project. If you are adding beading, be sure to avoid beading in the ¼" (6 mm) seam allowance.

8. Prepare for Construction

Once you have completed your embellishment, review the instructions for our seam variations on page 144 to determine your seam design of choice. Begin constructing the dress by pinning the center front panel to each of the side front panels, following the instructions for "pinning the middle" on page 19. Repeat this process for the Camisole Dress back.

9. Construct Dress

Thread your needle with button craft thread, "love your thread," and knot off (see pages 132–133). Using a straight stitch (see page 136), sew the pinned pieces together, starting at the top edge of one seam and stitching ¼" (6 mm) from the fabric's cut edges down to the bottom edge. Be sure to begin and end the seam by wrap-stitching (see page 144) its edges to secure them. Fell (see page 145) each seam by folding over the seam allowances to one side and topstitching them ⅛" (3 mm) from the cut edges (down the center of the seam allowances), using a straight stitch and wrap-stitching the seam. Repeat this process for each seam.

Next pin the shoulder seams with raw edges aligned, and sew the seams, following the instructions above for sewing the front and back panels. Note that you can either leave the shoulder seams floating (see page 144) or fold the allowances toward the back and fell them down the center. Pin the constructed front and back panels together at the side seams and follow the instructions above for sewing the panels together.

10. Bind Neckline and Armholes

Use the rotary cutter, cutting mat, and large plastic ruler to cut 1¼"- (3-cm-) wide strips of leftover fabric across the grain to use for binding the neckline and armholes. You will need approximately 80" (2 m) of cut strips for the binding. Use your iron to press each binding strip in half lengthwise, with the wrong sides together, being careful not to stretch the fabric while pressing it.

Starting at the center back neckline, encase the neckline's raw edge inside the folded binding, and baste the binding in place. When you need to add a new binding strip, simply overlap the strips' raw edges by about ½" (12 mm). Finally overlap the binding's raw edges at the center back by about ½" (12 mm), trimming any excess binding. Using the stretch stitch of your choice (see page 138), sew through all layers and down the middle of the binding. Repeat the process to finish each armhole. Remove or simply break the neckline and armhole basting stitches by pulling gently on one end of the thread. If some of the basting stitches are embedded in the binding, it is fine to leave them in place since the thread is broken and the stitches will not restrict the fabric's stretch.

Alabama Stitch Book

The first book we produced, *Alabama Stitch Book,* will always hold a favored place in my heart. It celebrates where we came from and the rich history that has become Alabama Chanin. It focuses on the story of cotton in our community and our early work using recycled T-shirts as a fabric source. It includes instructions for our classic Alabama Chanin appliqué embellishments along with twenty projects for home and wardrobe, among them, two of Alabama Chanin's most popular garments, the Swing Skirt and the Corset. The Swing Skirt will forever be known in our studio as the "A-79" since it was the 79th pattern we ever made. Its slight A-line shape has proven perfect for a variety of figures, and the four panels are easy to cut, embellish, and construct. For this reason, the Swing Skirt is a Studio Style DIY staple in a variety of lengths. Choose a comfortable fit with this garment, and you will find it to be a constant companion through your busy life. Add pockets (see page 28) or a border of a contrasting color at the bottom (see page 95) to vary the styling.

The Corset pattern started out as "A-09"—the 9th garment that we made. Like many great patterns, the style was modified and tweaked over the years to evolve into what, in the studio, we now call "A-368"—and some of our customers refer to as Wonder Alabama. Thanks to the give of cotton jersey and the strength of hand-made seams, this corset provides wonderful support and comfort, and fits and flatters womanly curves. Because of the support this corset offers, I suggest that you choose a smaller, tighter fit than you might for other garments. I have heard customers express concern about the hand-sewn seams breaking as they slip on the corset, but I always assure them that if you work the seams in two strands of our button craft thread (see page 132), as we suggest, they will not break. The button craft thread gives our garment strength and structure—as boning did in the corset's earlier iterations hundreds of years ago.

Before you start any of these projects, please review our overview of construction and embellishment techniques in Part 3, starting on page 126.

Corset and Swing Skirt Master Patterns

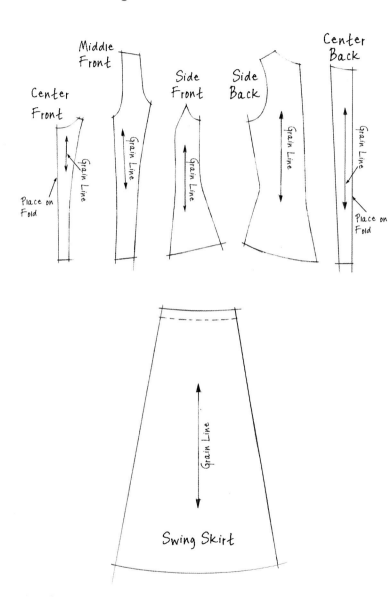

WRITING ON COTTON JERSEY

Over the years, we've used permanent markers for everything from transferring stencil designs (see page 146) to adding words or stories to quilts and garments, as on the Corset shown on the opposite page on which we wrote the following:

"If you can't fly then run, if you can't run then walk, if you can't walk then crawl, but whatever you do you have to keep moving forward."
—Martin Luther King, Jr.

Here are a few guidelines for writing on cotton jersey that we've developed through experience:

• We often construct our garments before we add the handwriting. This allows the writing to cross the finished seams and move unbroken around the neckline or body of a garment.

• Use tailor's chalk or a disappearing textile marker to define the area you want to embellish with writing.

• Print out the words or sayings you want to write in advance and look at each word before you apply it to your project. This has saved me many a misspelled word and slows me down so I can focus on my best penmanship.

• If you are writing on a single layer of fabric, place a second layer of scrap fabric underneath your writing. This keeps the layer you are working on from slipping and sliding as you write.

• Sometimes we embellish our written words by embroidering over them with embroidery floss. We try to match the color of the permanent marker and the color of embroidery floss.

• If something should go wrong, most commercial dry-cleaning chemicals will remove permanent marker from most cotton jersey fabrics. Alternatively, if you don't want your work to disappear, don't dry clean your finished piece.

Corset

Our most popular top, this garment is cut low in the front, the neckline and armholes are bound, and the back hem (measuring approximately 22½" [56 cm] from the center-back neck) is slightly longer than the front hem. Use the instructions on page 117 to raise or lower this neckline.

To make this piece, follow the instructions on page 70 for constructing the Camisole Dress, joining the corset panels as shown below. Take special care with the placement of the middle-front panels, since these two pieces are easy to switch and misplace, which will cause the hemline to be uneven. To avoid misplacing the panels, check that the grain lines (see page 135) on these two pieces follow the grain lines of the other front panels.

See the chart on page 174 for yardage requirements.

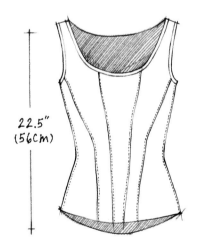

22.5"
(56cm)

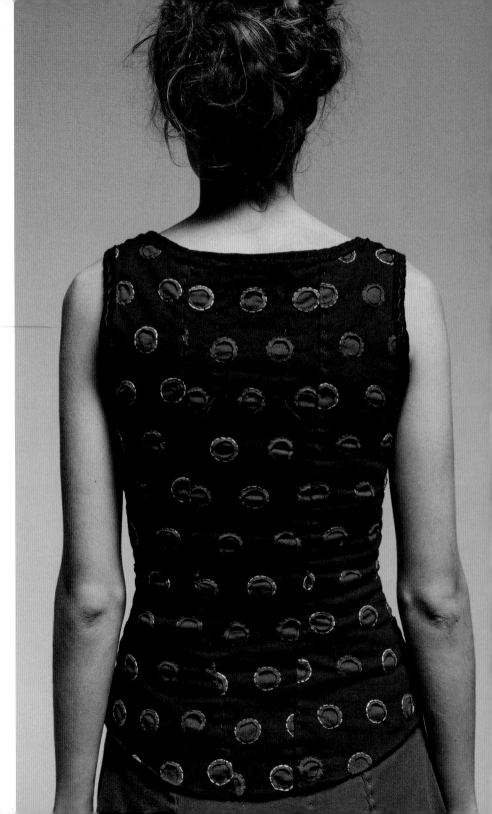

Swing Skirt

The A-Line Swing Skirt is a great addition to every wardrobe, whether sewn unadorned or elaborately embellished. This skirt is included in three lengths: 21" (53 cm), 24" (61 cm), and 26" (66 cm) from the waistband to the hem. The pattern is one simply shaped piece cut out four times, which can easily be altered, using the instructions for "Perimeter vs. Internal Alterations" on page 92. You can also enhance this skirt by working piping at the seams as shown for the top on page 27.

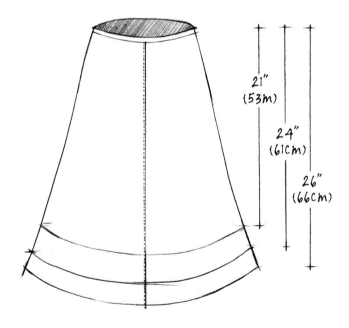

21"
(53m)

24"
(61cm)

26"
(66cm)

Swing Skirt and its variations

Swing Skirt Instructions

SUPPLIES

Basic sewing supplies listed on page 128

Swing Skirt pattern printed from this book's CD

60"- (1.5-m-) wide light- or medium-weight cotton-jersey fabric (see page 130) in one color, for top layer (see chart on page 174 for yardage needed)

60"- (1.5-m-) wide light- or medium-weight cotton-jersey fabric in a second color, for backing layer (optional)

1 yard (.9 m) of fold-over elastic (see page 129)

1. Cut Pattern and Fabric, and Prepare for Construction

Follow Steps 1–3 for the A-Line Dress on page 18 to prepare and cut your pattern, and cut the top-layer pieces and, for a double-layer garment, the backing-layer pieces. Then baste (see page 136) the waistline of each cut piece, and follow Steps 5–8 on page 19 to add stenciling and embellishment as desired and to prepare for construction.

2. Construct Skirt

Since all four skirt panels are identical, you can begin with any two pieces, aligning them and pinning the seams together following directions for the seam of your choice (see page 144). Remember to pin the pieces together by "working the middles" (see page 19), "love your thread" (see page 132), and use a wrap-stitch at the beginning and end of each seam (see page 144). Then repeat the process to join the remaining panels.

3. Bind Waistline

Using ⅞"- (2-cm-) wide fold-over elastic (see page 129) and starting at the skirt's center-back waistline, encase the waistline's raw edge with the folded elastic, basting the elastic in place as you work. Overlap the elastic's raw edges at the center back by about ½" (12 mm), and trim off any excess elastic. To sew the elastic in place permanently, use the stretch stitch of your choice (see page 138), stitching through all of the layers down the middle of the elastic.

PART 2

FIT + CUSTOMIZATION

Before adding a new garment style to a collection, we test the pattern for fit and appeal in its most basic version — without any embroidery or embellishment. Over the years, these simple garments have become an integral part of my personal wardrobe. They can be made with a single- or double-layer of fabric, and in a variety of colors and lengths to layer with more elaborately embellished pieces.

If you are happy with the fit of your basic garment, you are good to go. If it just needs a few small alterations, you may be able to mix and match the sizes already on the pattern (see page 88) or adjust the seams. For example, simply open up the seam approximately 3" (7.5 cm) beyond the area you want to alter, mark your new sewing line with a piece of tailor's chalk or a disappearing-ink fabric marker, and sew your new seam line for an improved new fit. But, if you want to make more significant changes, you will want to review the more involved customization techniques presented in this chapter.

On Sizing + Customization

When Alabama Chanin started, like every other fashion company, we developed sizing/grading standards that remain with us today. The term *grading standards* refers to the measurements between the individual sizes from XXS to XXL, or 0 to 22. We now base all of our garments in every collection on the standards that we set for our company more than a decade ago. And these are the standards we apply when making our patterns available to the home sewer.

The beauty of life is that, as human beings, we are all unique. And, furthermore, our unique bodies change over time—meaning that what fit me at age 20 does not fit three decades later. However, Alabama Chanin garments tend to fit a lot of different body shapes because they are made from cotton-jersey knit fabric, which stretches to accommodate. But, because we cannot accommodate every possibility within the collection, we are presenting our guidelines for sizing, re-sizing, and customizing here.

SIZE CHART

	XS	S	M	L	XL	XXL
SIZE	0–2	4–6	6–8	10–12	14–16	16–18
CHEST	28–30" (71–76 cm)	30–32" (76–81 cm)	32–34" (81–86 cm)	36–38" (91–96 cm)	40–42" (101–106 cm)	44–46" (112–117 cm)
WAIST	23–24" (58–61 cm)	25–26" (63.5–66 cm)	27–28" (68.5–71 cm)	30–32" (76–81 cm)	33–35" (84–89 cm)	35–36" (89–91.5 cm)
HIP	32–33" (81–84 cm)	34–35" (86–89 cm)	36–38" (91–96 cm)	38–39" (96–99 cm)	40–42" (101–106 cm)	43–44" (109.5–112 cm)

Note: When choosing your size, remember that cotton jersey stretches when worn. What begins as a snug dress will relax after only an hour of wearing.

Body Shapes

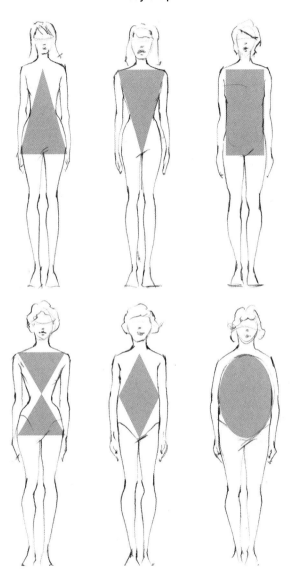

The most basic body shapes are triangle, inverted triangle, rectangle, hourglass, diamond, and oval.

Getting Ready to Customize

Patternmaking and pattern alteration generally involve moving shapes—both curved and linear—into other curved and linear shapes. For example, one could change a slightly curving bust line to a more robust curve to fit a more ample bosom, shorten the length of a rectangular-shaped skirt pattern to change the style, or increase the circumference of a sphere to add to a skirt's hip measurement. To get started with altering patterns, I recommend that you have the helpful tools on page 128 on hand.

Understanding the shape and size of your body is the first step in choosing, altering, or making a garment that fits well. Body shapes vary infinitely, but the most basic body shapes range generally from an inverted triangle form to an oval and from an hourglass shape to a rectangle—with every shape in between.

I love this quote from Adele P. Margolis, from her 1969 book, *How to Make Clothes That Fit and Flatter*, since it describes my own struggle with fit and body proportions as I have grown older:

There's no doubt about it! Slim figures are easier to dress. What figure faults they possess (and they do!) can more easily be hidden. What on earth can hide a bulge or a roll of fat except a "tent" dress or some variation of a maternity dress? Many a fitting problem would diminish with the loss of a few pounds and a little exercise. But not all! A weight loss alone will not solve fitting problems attributable to build or age. Were I, for example, to lose the twenty pounds that would bring me back to the skinny days of my youth, the problem of sloping shoulders, a pyramidal structure, a thickening waistline, and a sagging bosom would still plague me. But I would have a wider selection of styles available to me and with some adjustment they would look vastly better on me.

    If twenty pounds is an out-of-the-question weight loss for one who has lived enough years to consider her evening cocktail and a gourmet meal among the finer things in life, then at least one can think thin and try for ten. In the ensuing struggle, it's a comfort to know that it is better to fit the clothes you would like to wear than to make the clothes fit what you are—especially if what you are is anything less than great.

Measuring Your Body

To get started, use a standard cloth tape measure to take your measurements while standing barefoot and wearing your best undergarments or the undergarments you plan to wear under a special outfit (see "Finding the Perfect-Fitting Bra" on page 84). You may want to have a friend help with this process since there are some measurements that are difficult to take by yourself. Note that some of the measurements we have listed may not be necessary for basic pattern alterations, but if you think you will ever find yourself with a fitting challenge, it is a good idea to take all the measurements suggested. The average sewer will want to concentrate on the bust, waist, high hip, low hip, and lengths for skirts and/or sleeves.

Once you have decided to make a garment, compare your measurements to the measurements of the pattern pieces. This will help you understand how the garment will actually fit on your body and enable you to identify areas where you may want to make alterations. For example, you may want the garment's waist to be smaller or to have more ease in the hips or more room in the bust. Or the existing pattern measurements may seem just right for your body. If you do want want to make alterations, turn to page 90 to learn specific techniques for making them.

CIRCUMFERENCE

1. **Neck**—Measure at the fullest part of the neck.

2. **Chest**—Measure at the underarm and just above the breast.

3. **High bust**—Measure underneath the armpit but above the bust line.

4. **Bust**—Measure over the bust point (the nipple or fullest part of the bust) and straight across the back.

5. **Bust distance**—Measure from bust point to bust point.

6. **Waist**—Measure at the natural dip at the side or where you want the waistline of your garment to sit.

7. **High hip**—Measure at the top of the hip bone and approximately 3" (7.5 cm) below the waist. If this is a problem fit area for your body, you can take an additional measurement of how far the high hip sits below the waistline.

8. **Low hip**—Measure at the largest part of the hips and approximately 7" (17 cm) below the waist. If this is a problem fit area for your body, you can take an additional measurement of how far the low hip sits below the waistline.

9. **Bicep**—Measure at the largest part of the bicep.

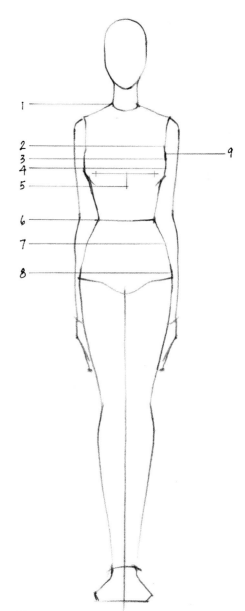

Name:
Date:

LENGTH

10. **Neck opening**—Measure from the center-front neck (just above the collar bone) to the desired neckline height.

11. **Shoulder to bust point**—Measure from the shoulder at the base of the neck to the bust point (nipple).

12. **Center front**—Measure from the center-front neck to the natural waist.

13. **Center back**—Measure from the base of the neck to the natural waist.

14. **Waist to high hip**—Measure from the waist to the top of the hip bone.

15. **Waist to low hip**—Measure from the waist to the widest part of the hip.

16. **Skirt length**—Measure from the waist to the desired length.

17. **Sleeve Length**—Measure from the shoulder point to the desired length.

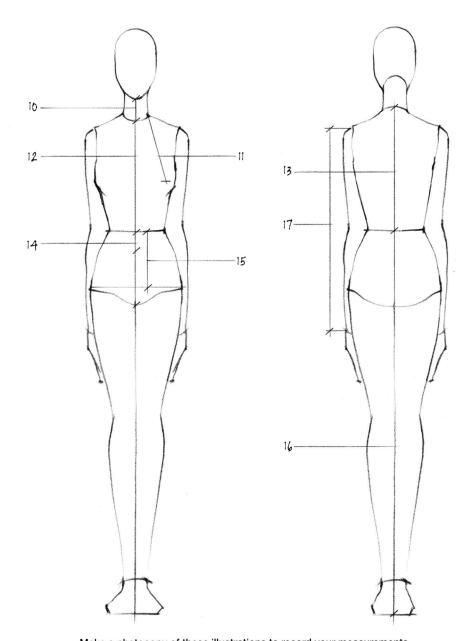

Make a photocopy of these illustrations to record your measurements.

Finding the Perfect-Fitting Bra

A bra that fits well can make you feel comfortable in whatever you wear–and can make the clothing you wear flatter your figure. If your bra is not right for your particular body shape, you may look like you have gained a few pounds, your posture can suffer, and your clothes may fall awkwardly on your frame.

We recommend that all women visit a store that offers a professional bra-fitting. Once you have been measured and know your proper bra size, try on different styles to learn which one flatters your body and is most comfortable. As with any garment, do not fixate on fitting into a particular size or shape. When buying a bra, always shop for your actual size; do not try to squeeze into smaller sizes hoping for better results. Be patient during the selection process.

If a bra fits correctly, it should not be painful or uncomfortable to wear. Most bras are sized according to two measurements: the band length (or measurement around the body, which is generally in the 30–40" (75–100 cm) range and designated in even numbers, such as 32, 34, 36, and so on); and the cup size (or volume of each breast), which is designated by a letter or multiples of that letter, starting with A.

The bra's band should carry approximately 80 percent of the weight of the breast—especially in larger sizes—with the straps that go over your shoulders supporting the remaining 20 percent of the weight. Measure your band size just under the breasts and around the back (see page 82). Generally speaking, you would add 2–3" (5–7.5 cm) to the band-width measurement to get your correct band size. Once you have calculated this measurement, try on several sizes in the range around this size to assess what feels right. Keep in mind that different brands and different styles within the same brand will fit differently. Breast shape may also change the way a style and size fits your individual body.

Most bras will have several rows of hook-and-eye closures at the back. Start wearing the bra you choose with the hooks on the largest settings. Bra bands stretch out after many wearing and washings, and you will reduce the size of the band with these hooks as you go through the life of the bra. However, sometimes you will also need these hooks for fit adjustments—for example, in some bras, a 36 may feel loose and a 34 too tight, and you can use the hooks to find the perfect fit. Or, if you are like me, you can gain or lose a few pounds over the course of a month, and the hooks will help you navigate these small changes. Hook-and-eye extensions are also available at better lingerie stores and are used to expand the fit range for women who may have a larger back span.

It helps to try on bras (and other undergarments) both while standing up and sitting down, so you can determine if you will be comfortable wearing them all day. If the bra band rides up on your back, the band is too large (loose) and you need to go down in the band size.

Determining your cup size is a little more difficult than band width, and preference also plays a big role. Bras come in a variety of cup formats and shapes—underwire cups, push-up, padded, sports bras, and a range of everything in-between—and you should take the time to determine what suits you best. Even with exacting measurements, you will still need to try on different styles to figure out which ones work for you.

For the cup size, measure yourself again at the fullest part of your breasts. If you own a non-padded bra that you love, take your measurement with your bra on—especially in the case of very large breasts that might "flatten" without the bra. The difference between your measurement at the bust apex and under the bust determines cup size.

While the chart at right is useful for determining the cup size, bra cup sizes also change as the band size increases, meaning that the volume of a particular cup size does not remain consistent as the band size changes. So, as you go up or down in band size, you may need to increase or decrease your cup size—for example, if you try on a 36C, and the cup size fits but the band is too loose and you go down in band size to a 34, you may actually need a 34D cup size to have about the same volume in the bra cup. Time to experiment and patience help in this selection process.

Once you have found a band and cup that fit perfectly, you will want to get a friend or salesperson to help you adjust the straps. A perfectly fitting strap should hold the cup without being so tight that you cannot move comfortably.

Tips for the perfect fit

• A bra should fit snugly under your breast but with enough ease to fit one or two fingers under the band comfortably. If you are pulling down the back strap or pulling up on the shoulder straps throughout the day, then the band size may be too big.

• If you are wearing an underwire bra, the wire coming up between the breasts should lie flat on the breast bone. If the wire between the breasts gapes or alternatively pokes your skin, try another band size.

• If you are wearing a bra without an underwire, you should have two separate breasts, not a "uni-boob."

• Your breast should fill the cup—that is, you should not have any extra fabric or room in the cup itself. If the cup gapes and the band feels fine, go down in the cup size. If you are spilling out of the cup, go up a cup size.

• Our bodies change as we age. So it makes sense that you probably should not be wearing the same undergarments at 50 that you wore at 18. A well-fitting undergarment can give you confidence to wear a greater variety of clothes.

CUP SIZE CHART

CUP SIZE DIFFERENCE	1" (2.5 cm)	2" (5 cm)	3" (7.5 cm)	4" (10 cm)
CUP SIZE	A	B	C	D

CUP SIZE DIFFERENCE	5" (12 cm)	6" (15 cm)	7" (17 cm)
CUP SIZE	DD or E	DDD or F	DDDD or G

Using Our Patterns

All three of our previous sewing books—*Alabama Stitch Book*, *Alabama Studio Style*, and *Alabama Studio Sewing + Design*—come with paper pattern sheets for the garments and accessories they feature so that home sewers and DIY enthusiasts can recreate them. Because of the size of these pattern sheets (which is determined by the book printer's machinery), some pattern pieces are broken into multiple segments and others are layered on top of one another; all of the patterns are nested with their various sizes together. As a result, it can take a bit of effort to use some of these patterns.

To streamline, *Alabama Studio Sewing Patterns* comes with a CD stocked with ready-to-print files for all the garments from our previous books and this one. The patterns can be emailed from your computer or brought to a copy/print shop and printed out on extra-large paper so that there is no joining or overlapping of the pattern pieces necessary. The overall printed size of the pattern paper might range from 24 x 36" (60 x 90 cm) for the Corset to multiple pages at 36 x 60" (90 x 150 cm) for the Long Fitted Dress. Each pattern sheet on the CD features a sizing square with the Alabama Chanin logo that should measure 2" (5 cm) when the pattern is printed at full size. Be sure to double check this measurement as soon as you receive your printout, and before cutting and working with your pattern.

There are wide-format printers on the market today that commonly print 36" (90 cm) and sometimes up to 44" (112 cm) wide and as long as the roll of paper that fits the machine. Look for a copy/print shop in your community that works with architects, who also have large-scale printing needs. Prices for printouts can vary widely from shop to shop, and it pays to take the time to research the best value available. If you cannot find a wide-format printer in your own community, there is a range of online printing services that will print digital files and ship to your door. When looking online, use search-word phrases like *large-scale printing* and/or *wide-format printing*. Please remember that Alabama Chanin patterns are copyrighted for individual home use only.

Alternatively, you can print a pattern at home by using a tiling program that breaks it up to fit on home-printer-sized paper. This process requires a lot of attention to detail and, in my experience, is not exact. It is not ideal, but I know it can work with some dedication and expertise.

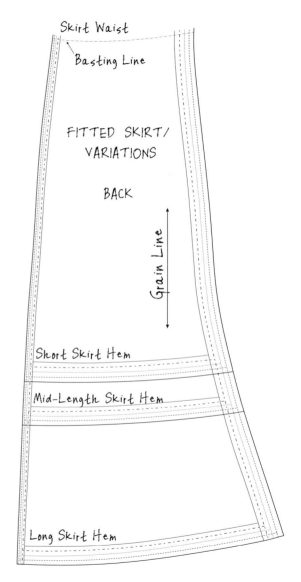

Nested pattern piece for Fitted Skirt

On the CD, you will find the following patterns in PDF form, ready for printing:

New patterns featured in this book
A-Line Top, A-Line Tunic, A-Line Dress, Long A-Line Dress, Classic Cardigan, Mid-Length Classic Jacket, Long Classic Coat, Short Wrap Skirt, Classic Wrap Skirt, Long Wrap Skirt

From *Alabama Studio Sewing + Design*
Fitted Top, Fitted Tunic, Short Fitted Dress, Long Fitted Dress, T-Shirt Top, Bolero, Short Fitted Skirt, Mid-Length Fitted Skirt, Long Skirt, Poncho

From *Alabama Studio Style*
Camisole Top, Camisole Tunic, Camisole Dress, Tank Top, Tank Tunic, Tank Dress, Gore Skirt

From *Alabama Stitch Book*
Corset, Swing Skirt

Mixing and Matching Pattern Sizes

If your body is like mine, your top is one pattern size, your waist another, and your hips a third size. In this book and on its CD, as is common in the sewing industry, you will find all the sizes for a given pattern nested together in each pattern piece, as in the facing illustration.

Note that the cutting lines for the various sizes are indicated by different line weights or combinations of dashes and dots. To avoid confusion when working with these patterns, familiarize yourself with the cutting lines for each size and also with the lines denoting grain line and basting.

To create a garment that is correctly sized for your body, you can use these nested patterns as a tool to improve fit by cutting different parts of a garment in different sizes—for example, cut your top and bust in a size Small, your waist in a size Extra Small, and your hip in a size Medium. Then use your straight ruler and curved pattern-making ruler to smooth the lines between the different sizes, as shown by the red line in the illustration at right. This approach will always be my favorite method of altering patterns since so much of the guesswork is eliminated when you can simply move from one size to another.

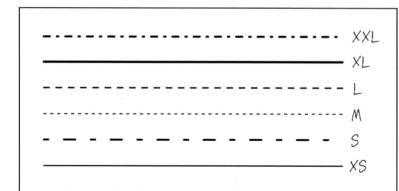

Cutting lines for different sizes

Nested Fitted Top

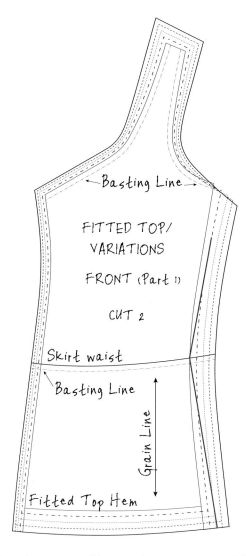

Basting Line

FITTED TOP/
VARIATIONS

FRONT (Part 1)

CUT 2

Skirt waist

Basting Line

Grain Line

Fitted Top Hem

Nested patterns enable you to improve a garment's fit by cutting various areas in different sizes. Here, the red cutting line moves from a size Small at the bust to Extra Small at the waist to Medium at the hips.

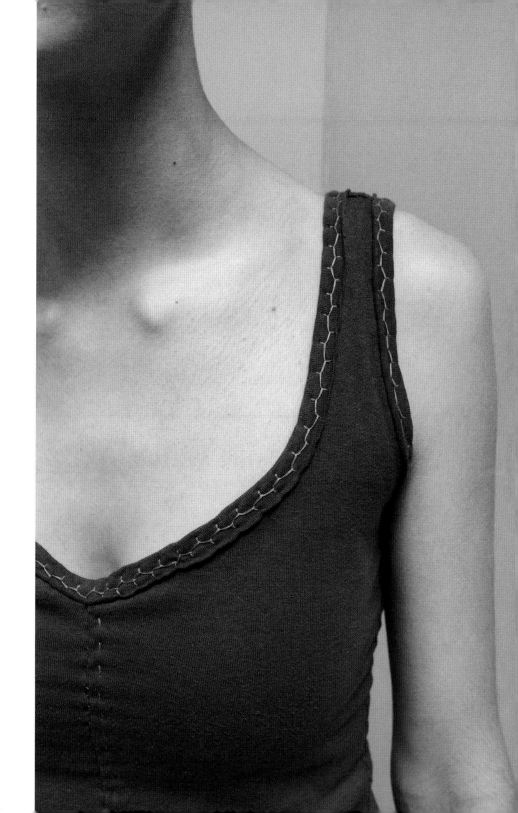

Altering Paper Patterns

When we want to make significant changes to a paper pattern and cannot simply follow different line sizes on the existing paper pattern (as described on page 88), we make an adjustment either externally (on the perimeter of paper patterns; see page 93) or internally (on the interior of paper patterns; see page 96). Making these adjustments to a paper pattern is a simple matter of drawing and redrawing the pattern lines to specific measurements. Below are basic guidelines to keep in mind as you work.

1. Collect the tools listed on page 128, and clear a work surface. At Alabama Chanin, we use tall tables, so we can work standing upright since we find it easier to manipulate patterns this way, and it seems to put less stress on the lower back. But you should choose a working setup that is readily available and feels most comfortable for you.

2. Review your pattern sheet, and identify all the pattern pieces.

3. Choose the best size (or sizes) for your body (see "Mixing and Matching Pattern Sizes" on page 88 for working with multiple sizes in one pattern piece).

4. Trace the pattern onto a clean sheet of blank paper or gridded pattern paper to make the alterations instead of working directly on your paper pattern original since, depending on your skill level, it may take several tries to get a pattern's curves and lines exactly as you want them. Keep your original paper pattern for later use and to review during your pattern work. Use paper scissors to cut out your pattern pieces.

5. Identify the changes you want to make to the pattern, and note those changes directly on your traced pattern pieces, so that you have a detailed description of the changes you made to the original pattern.

6. Using your patternmaking tools and the directions that follow for each type of alteration in this chapter, alter your paper patterns as desired directly on the traced pattern pieces. Be sure to check or re-establish the grain line on each pattern piece, as explained on the facing page.

7. The best rule of thumb when making pattern alterations is to go slowly, measure twice, and cut once. When ready, cut out your finished pattern piece, and check it for accuracy. Tape extra pieces of pattern paper below your pattern piece as needed to make any additional pattern alterations to enlarge the pattern pieces. Retrace your altered pattern onto another piece of paper if you are making extensive changes to the pattern. If you are making only minor changes to the pattern and it does not need to be retraced, use your altered pattern to cut out your project fabric.

8. Once you have altered the new paper pattern, use an ink pen to label the name of the garment and pattern piece on each individual piece. It is also helpful to add the date and notes about the alterations you made to the pattern. Use a manila envelope to keep pattern pieces together; add a sketch or note on the outside of the envelope to make organization easy.

9. Since this stage of the process seems to make most people nervous, keep in mind that this is just a piece of paper that can easily be redrawn from your original cut pattern. Altering the pattern should be an entertaining, pleasant experience. Don't worry that something will go wrong; in many cases, it will—but it will not be irrevocable.

Reestablishing the Grain Line

The term *grain line* refers to a straight line indicated on all garment pattern pieces that should be used to position, or lay out, each pattern piece on the project fabric so that the pattern's grain line aligns with the grain of the fabric. To learn how to identify the grain line on cotton jersey, see page 135. Both knitted and woven fabrics have a grain line that run parallel to the selvedge, or finished edge. The term *cross grain* refers to the line that is perpendicular to the selvedge of your fabric.

In knit fabric, the cross grain stretches much more than the grain line. Our Alabama Chanin patterns are designed with this in mind. It is important to line up the grain line on your pattern with your fabric's grain line so you retain the maximum stretchability and produce the best-fitting, most comfortable garment possible.

When you are altering your paper pattern, always check and reestablish your grain line on the altered pattern before cutting your fabric.

Reestablishing altered pattern's grain line

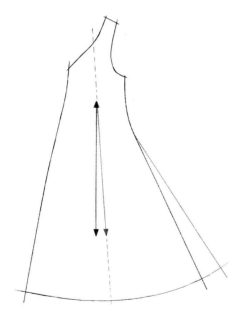

Reestablish grain line on altered pattern by folding pattern in half across its width, with edges touching and fold line perpendicular to hem. Fold line becomes new grain line.

Checking grain line on garment with princess seams

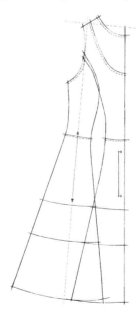

Reestablish grain line on altered princess-style garment by laying pattern pieces close together and drawing grain line perpendicular to imaginary line drawn across shoulder.

PERIMETER VS. INTERNAL ALTERATIONS

Pattern pieces can be altered either at their edges, or perimeter, or they can be altered internally within the body of the given piece(s). Small increases or decreases in pattern sizes—of 2" (5 cm) or less—can be made easily at the paper pattern's perimeter, and these are the easiest adjustments to make to a pattern. Perimeter changes of more than 2" (5 cm) can alter the shape of a pattern piece. For example, if you add 5" (12 cm) to the hem of a dress (as shown in the illustration at right below), the garment's final silhouette will be much wider at the sweep, or hem's circumference. For this reason, we recommend using the perimeter method only for changes of 2" (5 cm) or less at the pattern's edges. For larger changes of more than 2" (5 cm), we suggest making internal pattern alterations. Keep in mind that when adding a perimeter change to patterns cut on the fold, your addition will add double the measurement—so proceed cautiously when working with pieces cut on the fold.

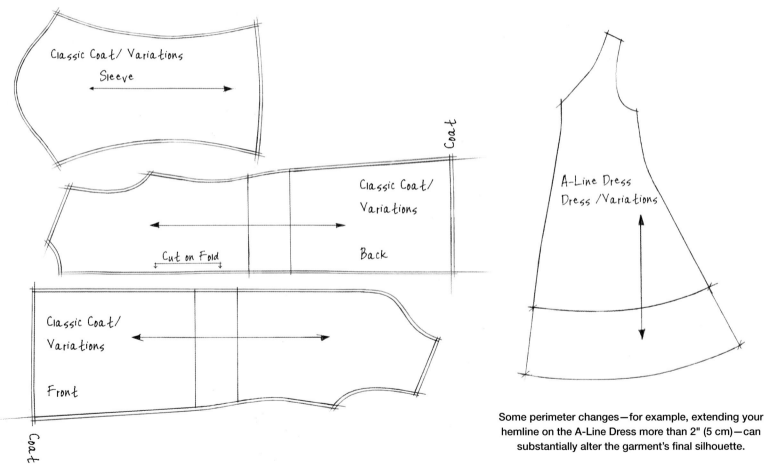

Classic Coat (page 30) with perimeter changes all around

Some perimeter changes—for example, extending your hemline on the A-Line Dress more than 2" (5 cm)—can substantially alter the garment's final silhouette.

INTERNAL PATTERN ALTERATIONS

Unequal Perimeter Changes

Remember that perimeter changes do not need to be equal throughout the length or width of the paper pattern piece. For example, you can add to one end of a paper pattern edge and taper to nothing at the other end.

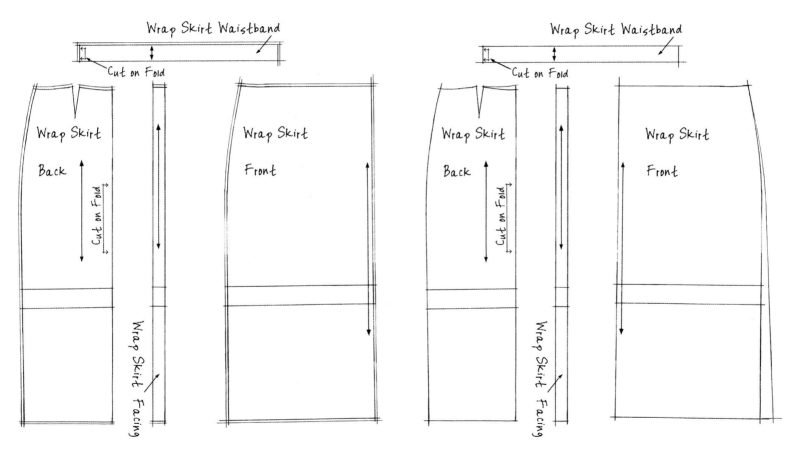

Wrap Skirt with equal perimeter changes on front, back, and waistband

Wrap Skirt front pattern piece on right side of illustration shows an unequal perimeter change beginning at hem and tapering to nothing at high hip. Wrap Skirt back pattern piece on left side shows unequal perimeter change at waist, with alteration tapering to nothing at dart.

Unpaired Perimeter Changes

Note that perimeter alterations do not have to be made in pairs. For example, you may want to add to the width of the garment in the front but not in the back if your front tends to be larger than your back.

Perimeter Changes on Sleeves and Armholes

However, note that if you add to the underarm side seam of a pattern with a sleeve, you must also add to the sleeve seam corresponding to the enlarged armhole.

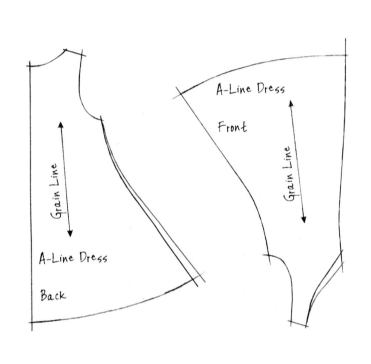

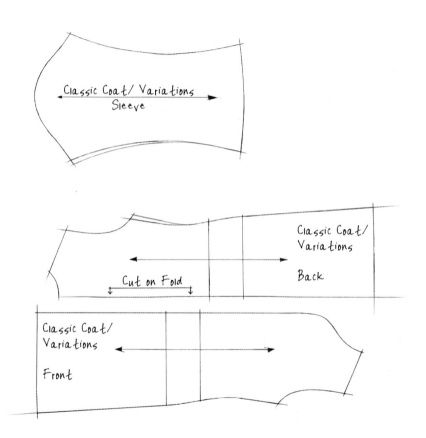

A-Line Tunic with perimeter changes only on back side edge and front neckline

Altering sleeve on back seam allowance requires matching this perimeter change on back pattern's armhole, as shown here on Classic Coat pattern.

ADDING BORDERS

It's easy to add a border to the hem of any garment. This technique can be used when you want to lengthen a garment or simply add a new design element.

1. Measure desired border's height from side seam and center front or back. Draw border's height and length on pattern paper.

2. Cut out border pattern, making sure that shape of pattern's top edge matches garment's bottom edge.

3. Add ¼" (6 mm) seam allowance to top of border pattern.

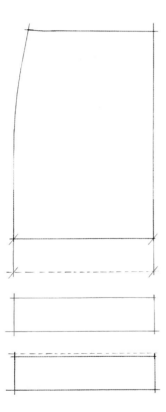

Creating a border for Wrap Skirt

INTERNAL PATTERN ALTERATIONS

Making pattern alterations of 2" (5 cm) or more is best done internally within the body of the pattern piece rather than at its perimeter edges. Internal pattern alterations are done either by slashing (cutting) the pattern piece fully or partially and spreading the cut edges to enlarge the pattern piece or by slashing and overlapping the cut edges (also called *tucking*) to reduce the pattern piece. Note that when you only partially slash a pattern piece rather than slashing the piece fully in two, you will leave one pattern edge intact that becomes a pivot edge. You can then spread or overlap the slashed sections below (or above) the pivot edge to make your alteration and leave the pivot edge itself unchanged from the original pattern.

Slashing and spreading or overlapping can be used to make simple changes to any pattern piece, including at the bust, waist, and/or in the length. These changes can be made horizontally (perpendicular to the grain line) to lengthen or shorten a pattern piece or vertically (normally following the grain line) to enlarge or reduce the width of a pattern piece. Making changes with internal pattern alterations helps retain the garment's original silhouette (since the pattern's outer edges generally remain intact). For example, you can lengthen the hem by 5" (12 cm), as shown at below right, by slashing and spreading to end up with the same sweep (hem circumference), as compared to lengthening the garment with the perimeter method (see page 92), which adds to the final sweep.

Partially slashing a pattern piece creates a pivot edge.

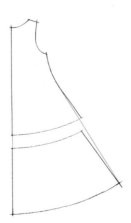

You can lengthen A-Line Dress 5" (12 cm) by slashing and spreading.

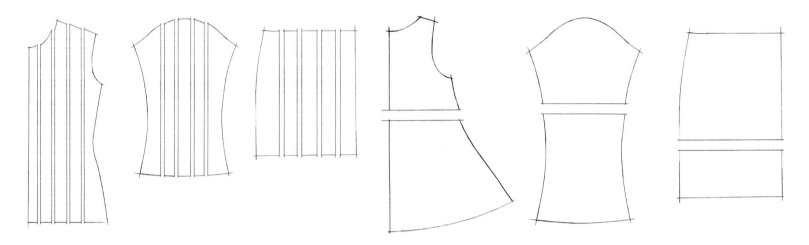

Fully slashing and evenly spreading pattern pieces enlarges them all over in width and length.

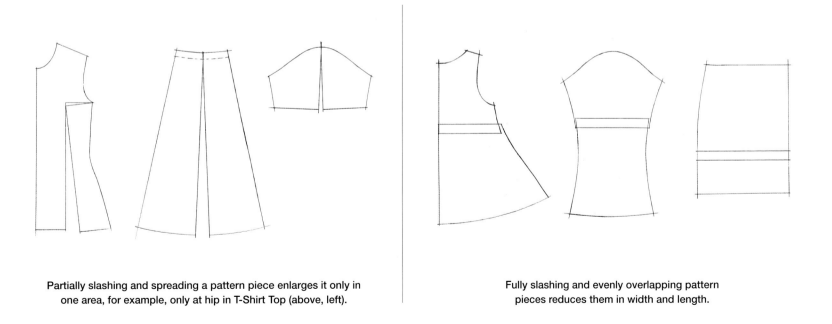

Partially slashing and spreading a pattern piece enlarges it only in one area, for example, only at hip in T-Shirt Top (above, left).

Fully slashing and evenly overlapping pattern pieces reduces them in width and length.

ALTERING THE WAISTLINE

To add 1" (2.5 cm) to the waist of a garment, you will first need to know how many seams intersect the garment's waistline, and, in most cases, you will want to distribute the 1" (2.5 cm) addition evenly around the entire garment. (Note that darts at the waistline should be left intact and the alterations made only to the seam lines.) For example, our Fitted Dress (see page 58) has four seams around its circumference. Each of these seams is made of two pieces of fabric, which means there are two seam allowances for each seam, or, in this case, a total of eight seam allowances around the waist. Dividing the total 1" (2.5 cm) increase by eight seam allowances means that, in order to distribute the 1" (2.5 cm) increase evenly around the garment, you will need to add $1/8$" (3 mm) to each seam allowance, as shown in the illustration.

It is important to take the time to check your math because a slight variation in a garment with many seam allowances like our Gore Skirt (see page 67), which has six panels equaling 12 seam allowances, can mean a substantial change in sizing overall. For example, if you miscalculate even $1/8$" (3mm) on 12 seam allowances, you will wind up with a waist that is $1\frac{1}{2}$" (4 cm) larger (or smaller) than you intended. This same need for good math holds true when constructing a garment: For a perfect fit, it is imperative that you take the same care when sewing your seams since a slight variation in the seam's allowances can create large changes in the fit of your garment.

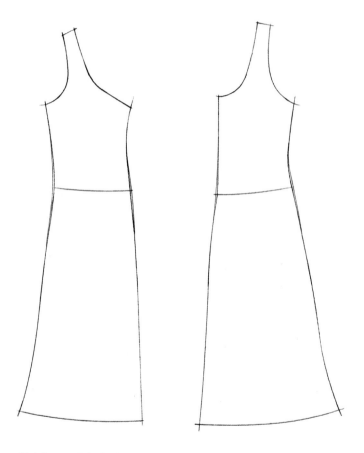

Dividing total desired increase by number of seam allowances yields increase needed at each seam allowance. Adding $1/8$" (3mm) to each of eight seam allowances (remember, each seam is made of two pieces of fabric) at waistline of Fitted Dress adds 1" (2.5 cm) overall.

To alter the waistline at the perimeter

1. For an alteration of 2" (5 cm) or less at the waist, prepare your paper pattern pieces as outlined on page 90.

2. Determine how much you want to increase or decrease the waistline.

3. Divide the increase or decrease by the number of seam allowances in your garment that intersect the waistline (remember that each edge sewn into a seam has a seam allowance, and hence each seam has two seam allowances). So, for example, if you want to increase the waist by 1" (2.5 cm) and your garment has two seams, you will increase each seam allowance by ¼" (6 mm) (2 seams = 4 seam allowances, and 1" [2.5 cm] ÷ 4 = ¼" [6 mm]). Note that if your waistline has darts, leave them intact and unaltered, and make the needed alterations working only with the seam allowances.

4. Locate the waistline on your paper pattern piece, and draw a pencil line to mark the waist if your pattern does not already have the waistline marked.

5. Carefully note in pencil on the pattern piece(s) the amount determined in Step 3 that you want to add to or subtract from each seam allowance at the waistline.

6. Mark the actual alteration at each seam.

7. Using your straight ruler or pattern curves, draw a smooth line from your newly altered waistline to re-join the original pattern line on either side of each alteration (and if you are enlarging the seams, tape an extra piece of pattern paper at each seam allowance, if needed, to redraw the new seam allowance).

8. Test your pattern in fabric by making a basic unembellished garment. Note that increasing or decreasing the width of your pattern may affect the fabric yardage needed.

Adding to and subtracting from waistline at perimeter

Camisole Dress

Fitted Skirt   T-Shirt Top

To adjust the waistline internally

1. For an alteration of more than 2" (5 cm) at the waist, prepare your pattern pieces as outlined on page 90.

2. Determine how much you want to increase or decrease the waistline.

3. Determine how many pattern pieces you want to alter internally. To keep the same garment shape, alter all of your pattern pieces equally (in the case of princess seams, see page 110 for more information). To adjust the width of a single pattern piece (for example, to reduce the size of a front panel to keep the garment's lines positioned symmetrically under the bust), write the amount of change to be added or subtracted on that piece.

4. Draw a vertical line on the pattern piece (which would generally match the grain line) at the point you want to increase or decrease the width.

5. Cut the pattern piece in half fully or partially at the vertical line.

6. To increase the waistline, add an additional piece of paper behind your two cut pieces, separate the two pieces by the amount of the desired increase from Step 3, and tape the cut pieces securely to the backing layer of paper. To reduce the waistline, overlap the two cut pieces by the amount of the desired decrease, and tape the overlap securely in place. Note that, in a dress, this method can also be used to alter the bust line and hips.

7. Review the perimeter of each altered piece to make sure that no further adjustments need to be made to correct a waistline, neckline, or armhole.

8. Using your straight ruler or pattern curves, draw a smooth line from your altered waistline to re-join the original pattern line on either side of the alteration.

9. Test your pattern in fabric by making an unembellished basic garment. Note that increasing or decreasing the width of your pattern may affect the fabric yardage needed.

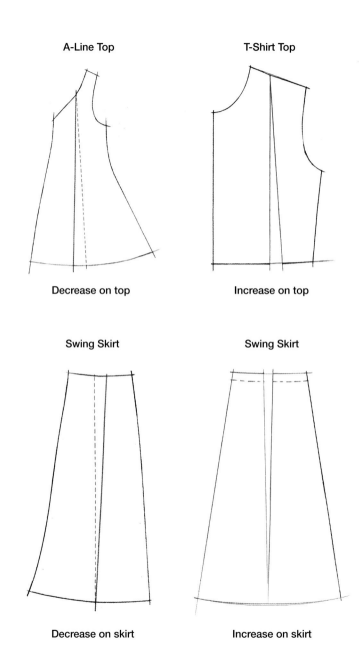

A-Line Top

T-Shirt Top

Decrease on top

Increase on top

Swing Skirt

Swing Skirt

Decrease on skirt

Increase on skirt

ALTERING DARTS

Darts are pattern devices used to remove fabric from various areas of a design to shape the garment to fit the body's curves. Darts can be used singly, in pairs, and, in some designs, in multiples. While most Alabama Chanin patterns do not have darts since the stretch of our cotton-jersey fabric generally eliminates the need for them, the new Wrap Skirt on page 36 does have two darts on the back pattern piece to help provide shaping for the buttocks.

If you are having trouble with fit in a given area, you can also try using one or more darts to solve the problem. For example, you can add a dart to our T-Shirt Top (on page 45) to take out some of the excess fabric around the armhole if it seems too large (remembering that you also have to make a corresponding alteration to the sleeve if your pattern calls for one).

Working with darts is simple but does take a little while to understand and is sometimes considered a more advanced pattern technique. But once you master the technique described below, you may want to add darts to every garment you make or own if you have hard-to-fit curves.

Where and why to use darts:

Bust line—Darts at the bust line are designed to point to the bust apex (the bust point, or nipple) and provide shape for the bosom. A dart can start at various points on the garment—at the side seam, armhole, shoulder, waistline, or, in some cases, the center-front seam (if there is one). In each case, the dart will angle from the starting point toward the bust apex.

A princess seam (see page 110) is a variation on a bust dart since the seam itself is shaped to contour the fabric in the bust area.

Waistline—Darts at the waist are designed to help the front of a skirt or dress lie flat across the stomach and to add shape and contour the back of the skirt or dress above the buttocks. Based on the measurement from your waist to your high or low hip, you may want to change the lengths of your waistline darts.

Take care when making changes to a paper pattern that will affect the pattern's darts. Slashing and spreading or overlapping the cut parts of a pattern (see Internal Pattern Alterations on page 96) can change the size of a dart, but you can easily redraw the dart by following the steps on page 102.

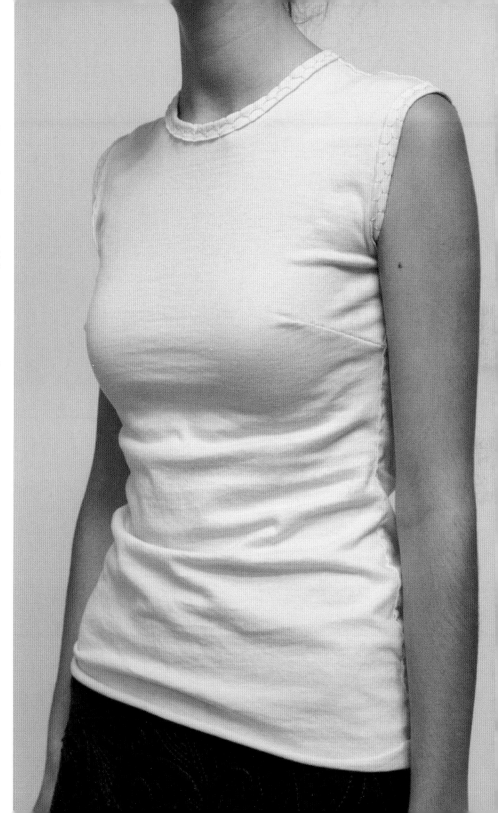

Drawing or repositioning a dart

1. Find the dart apex on your pattern, which will be the point of the original dart. If you are adding a new dart, the dart apex will be the fullest part of the curve you are fitting, for example, the bust point.

2. Measure the length of the dart on the original pattern. If you are adding a new dart, determine and mark the apex for the new dart on your pattern, and then measure the new dart's length from starting point to apex.

3. Measure the dart opening on the original pattern, or, in the case of a new dart, determine the dart's opening width, including ¼" (6 mm) for each of the dart's two seam allowances and tapering to between ⅛" (3 mm) and ¹⁄₁₆" (2 mm) at the dart point.

4. Mark the dart opening on your new pattern, and draw a straight line with your ruler from the dart apex to one side of the dart opening. Then repeat the process for the dart's other side.

Darts as Tool for Shaping Garments

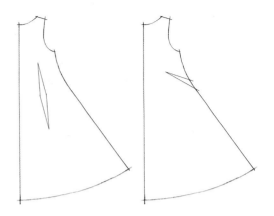

Darts can be positioned at various places on garment patterns to contour their shape.

Drawing a Dart from Scratch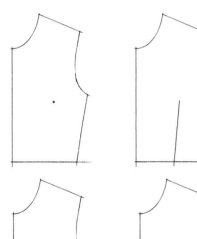

Repositioning a Dart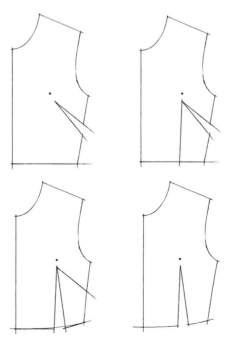

Dart line is transferred from paper pattern to fabric, then cut.

Sewn dart, with seam allowance tapering from ¼" (6 mm) at
side edge to between ⅛" (3 mm) and 1/16" (2 mm) at apex.

Possible dart lines show that bust line
darts can start at various points on side
seam, armhole, shoulder, or waistline.

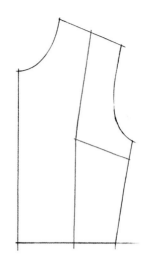

Adding a princess seam dart
(or additional seam)

Darts at back waist or side seam can shape skirt's waist and hips.

ALTERING THE HIPS

It is possible to alter the width of a garment at the high or low hip without alter-ing the waistline. As with altering the waistline, to alter the pattern at the hips, divide the overall amount of change needed by the number of seam allowances at the hip line in order to spread the change evenly across the pattern. (Note that if your pattern has darts at the hip line, leave them intact and make the needed alterations only at the seam lines.)

To adjust the hips at the perimeter

1. For changes of 2" (5 cm) or less at the hips, prepare your pattern pieces as outlined on page 90.

2. Determine the amount you want to increase or decrease the high hip and low hip, keeping in mind that you may not want to alter them both by the same amount.

3. Divide the desired increase or decrease by the number of seams in the garment's high hip and low hip (remembering that each seam has two seam allowances). For example, if you want to decrease your high hip by 2" (5 cm) overall and there are two seams in the pattern's high-hip area, you will need to decrease each seam allowance by ½" (12 mm) (2 seams = 4 seam allowances, and 2" [5 cm] ÷ 4 = ½" [12 mm]).

4. Locate the high and low hip on your pattern piece, and pencil a line to indicate both the high and low hips (some patterns may already have a line indicating one or both points on the hips).

5. Carefully note in pencil on the pattern pieces to be altered, the amount determined in Step 3 to add to or delete from each seam.

6. Mark the actual alteration on each seam at both the high and low hip lines.

7. Using your straight ruler and/or pattern curves, draw a smooth line from your newly altered hip line to re-join the pattern's hip line above and below each alteration.

8. Test your pattern in fabric by making an unembellished basic garment. Note that increasing or decreasing the width of your pattern may affect the fabric yardage needed.

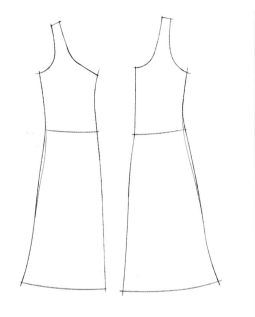

Subtracting from side seams

Adding to side seams

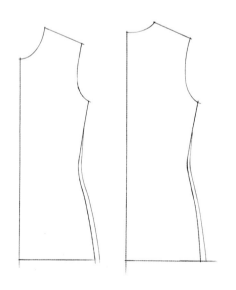

Adding to side seams

To alter the hips internally

1. For alterations of more than 2" (5 cm) to the hips, prepare your pattern pieces as outlined on page 90.

2. Determine how much you want to increase or decrease high hip and low hip. You may not want to alter each measurement by the same amount.

3. Determine how many pattern pieces you want to alter internally. Divide the total of the increase/decrease from Step 2 by the number of pattern pieces you want to alter. Often you will want to alter all of the pieces equally; you may want to make an exception if, for example, you have consistent fit issues or want to change the placement of seam lines. The result of your calculation is the amount you will adjust each seam to spread the alteration evenly across the hip line.

4. Draw the slash lines on your pattern piece(s).

5. Locate the high and low hip on your pattern piece, and draw pencil lines to indicate their position. Some patterns may already have a line indicating one or both points on the hips.

6. Cut the pattern piece fully or partially in half on the vertical slash lines. See the discussion of a pivot edge on page 96.

7. To increase the size of the hip line, add a piece of paper behind the two fully or partially cut sections of the pattern piece, separate the cut pieces by the amount of the desired increase from Step 3, and securely tape the cut pieces to the backing paper. To reduce the width of the hip line, overlap the two fully or partially cut pattern pieces by the desired decrease, and tape the overlapped pieces securely in place.

8. Review the perimeter of each altered pattern piece to make sure that no further alterations need to be made to correct a waistline, neckline, or armhole that is affected by the internal changes.

9. Using your straight ruler or pattern curves, draw a smooth line from your altered hip line to re-join the original pattern on either side of alterations.

10. Test your pattern in fabric by making an unembellished basted garment. Increasing or decreasing pattern width may affect yardage needed.

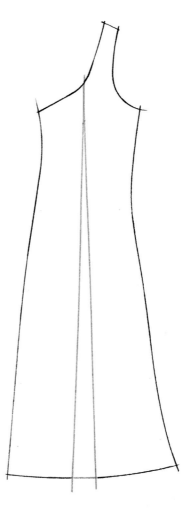

Adding to hip internally by spreading slash
(overlapping slash would subtract from hip)

Adding Seams to Adjust the Fit

You can also alter the size and shape of a waist or hip line by adding one or more seams to your pattern. For example, you can cut your pattern in half, as shown below on our Swing Skirt from page 73. Once you have cut the paper pattern piece at the desired spot, add or subtract the desired amount to each cut edge, and then add a seam allowance to both cut edges (taping pattern paper behind the cut edges to draw new seam allowances if you are enlarging the pattern).

Swing Skirt pattern cut in half

New pattern pieces with added width

New pattern pieces with
added seam allowences

Finished altered pattern pieces

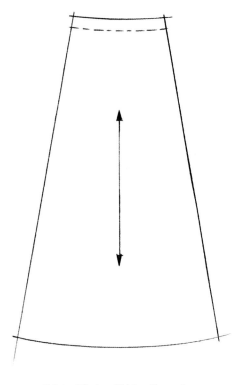

Original Swing Skirt pattern piece

SLASH AND SPREAD TO CREATE A FULLER SWEEP (HEM CIRCUMFERENCE)

To create a playful sweep at the hem of any of our skirt patterns, trace your pattern on pattern paper, and cut it out. Use your pattern-making tools (see page 128) to make multiple slash lines (see page 96) from the hem to the waistline of this skirt pattern. Spread the hem of the skirt apart, while keeping the waistline exactly the same measurement, as shown in the illustration at the far right top, which creates a wider pattern piece at the hem and retains the fit at the waistline.

Tape the slashed-and-spread pattern pieces to another piece of pattern paper, and trace your new pattern, as shown in the illustration at left below.

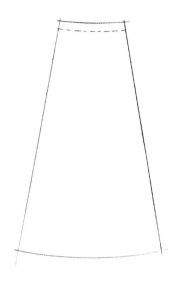

Swing Skirt pattern

Swing Skirt pattern slashed
and spread to alter its sweep

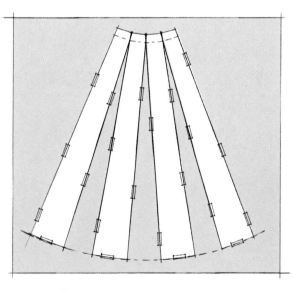

Slashed-and-spread pattern taped to
paper to trace and make new pattern

New pattern

ALTERING THE BUST LINE

The bust is one of the more difficult areas of the body to fit since each woman has her own shape, size, and preferences. Regardless of individual differences, a beautifully fitting bust line starts with a good undergarment (see page 84), and changing the undergarment can substantially change the garment's fit. For this reason, I recommend that you find a store in your community that has undergarment specialists who can help you. If you are shopping for or working on a garment for a special event, begin by choosing the perfect undergarment, and *then* work outward—keeping in mind that an undergarment that is too tight or too loose will show through your finished garment.

Since our cotton-jersey fabric is extremely forgiving and none of our top or dress patterns include bust darts (though they can be added), some of the more challenging pattern adjustment work has been eliminated. To achieve the best results, you may want to incorporate more than one of the alterations below. (In general, it is best to leave any darts in your pattern unchanged and to make your alterations only on the seam lines.)

To alter the bust at the perimeter

1. Note that we only use this technique on its own for alterations of less than 2" (5 cm) total at the bust. If we want to alter the bust by more than 2" (5 cm) total, we achieve this by altering both internally and at the perimeter. Prepare your pattern pieces as outlined on page 90.

2. Determine how much you want to increase or decrease the bust line.

3. Divide the desired increase or decrease by the number of seams in your garment. For example, if you want to increase the bust by 1" (2.5 cm) overall and your garment has four seams, you will add ⅛" (3 mm) to each seam allowance (4 seams = 8 seam allowances, and 1" [2.5 cm] ÷ 8 = ⅛" [3 mm]). Note that you can increase or decrease the pattern at the center front, side seams, or both places.

4. Locate the bust line on your pattern piece, and draw a line that corresponds with the bust across the width of your pattern piece.

5. Carefully note on the pattern piece(s) to be altered the amounts that you want to add to or delete from each seam.

6. At the bust line on each seam, add or subtract the amount determined in Step 3, marking the actual alteration in pencil on your pattern.

7. Using a straight ruler and/or pattern curves, draw a smooth line from your pattern's altered bust line on each altered piece to re-join the original pattern line on either side of each alteration.

8. Test your pattern in fabric by making an unembellished basic garment. Note that increasing or decreasing the width of your pattern may affect the fabric yardage needed.

Note: Extending or shortening the bust at center front and/or center back may lower or raise your neckline. Compensate for your alteration by adjusting your neckline and/or straps.

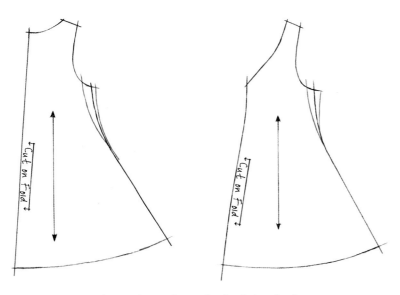

Increasing or decreasing bust at perimeter

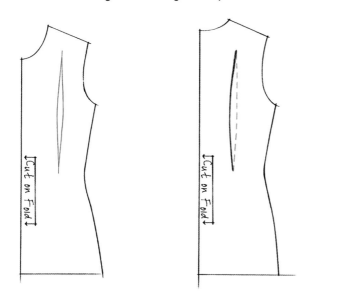

Increasing and decreasing bust internally (shown at left on garment front and at right on garment back)

To alter the bust internally

1. Note that we only use this technique on its own for alterations of less than 2" (5 cm) total at the bust. If we want to alter the bust by more than 2" (5 cm) total, we achieve this by altering both internally and at the perimeter. Prepare your pattern pieces as outlined on page 90.

2. Determine how much you want to increase or decrease the bust.

3. Determine how many pattern pieces you want to alter internally: To keep the same lines and proportions in your finished garment as on the original pattern, alter all of your pattern pieces. To adjust the width of a single pattern piece, choose the individual piece you want to alter, keeping in mind that this will change where the seams fall on your body in the finished garment. Write the amount of change to be added to each piece you want to alter.

4. Draw a vertical line on the pattern piece(s) to be altered (the line will usually match the grain line) at the point where you want to increase or decrease the bust's width.

5. Cut the pattern piece fully or partially in half at the vertical line.

6. To increase the width, add an additional piece of paper behind your two cut pieces, separate the cut pieces by the amount of the desired increase from Step 3, and tape the cut pieces securely to the backing paper. To reduce the width of the piece, overlap the two cut pieces by the amount of the desired decrease from Step 3, and tape the overlapped pieces securely in place. Note that in a dress, this method will also alter the waistline.

7. Review the perimeter of each altered piece to make sure that no further alterations are needed to correct a waistline, neckline, or armhole.

8. Using your straight ruler and/or pattern curves, draw a smooth line from your altered bust line to re-join the original pattern line on either side of each alteration.

9. Test your pattern in fabric by making an unembellished basic garment. Note that increasing or decreasing the width of your pattern may affect the fabric yardage needed.

ALTERING THE BUST (OR WAIST) ON PRINCESS SEAMS

Princess seams are long curving seams built into a garment to add shaping that closely follows a woman's figure. These seams are sewn into the front and/or back of a garment and usually extend from the armhole, directly over the bust point, past the waist and hips, and all the way to the hem. The curve of the princess seam lines—used in pairs—determines the shape of the bust, waist, hips, and, as it descends to the hem, the garment's sweep (or hem circumference). Straighter princess lines produce a more fitted sheath, while wider princess lines in a skirt create more volume, as on our Camisole Dress from *Alabama Studio Style*.

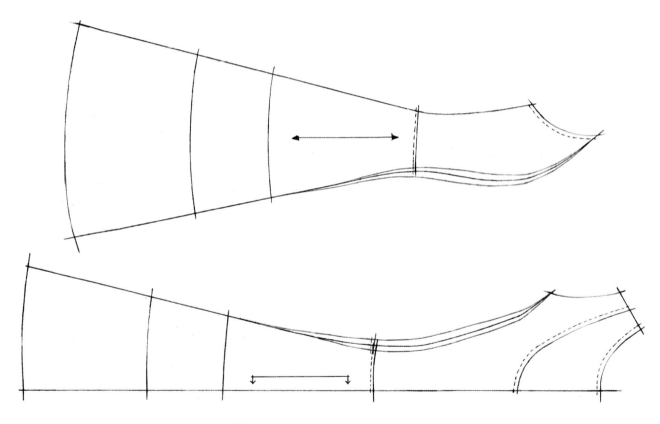

Adding and subtracting at princess seams

Alter the bust and/or waist on princess seams as follows:

1. Prepare your pattern pieces as outlined on page 90.

2. Determine how much you want to increase or decrease the bust and/or waistline.

3. Divide the amount of the increase or decrease by the number of seam allowances in your garment (remembering that each seam has two seam allowances).

4. Locate the bust and waistline on your pattern piece, and draw horizontal lines at the bust and waist levels across the width of your pattern piece.

5. Carefully note on each pattern piece to be altered the amount that you want to add to or subtract from each seam or seam allowance.

6. Mark the desired alteration at the bust and waistline on each seam.

7. Using your straight ruler and/or pattern curves, draw a smooth line from your alteration to re-join the original pattern line on either side of each alteration.

8. Test your pattern in fabric by making an unembellished basic garment. Note that increasing or decreasing the width of your pattern may affect the fabric yardage needed.

ALTERING PRINCESS SEAMS

Modified princess seams can start at the shoulder rather than the armhole (see the illustration below). These seams—as in our Camisole and Tank dresses from *Alabama Studio Style*—require special attention when making alterations. Since the curved pattern lines correspond to the bust and waist, you can make these changes at the same time, working most easily with perimeter alterations (see page 93) to the pattern pieces.

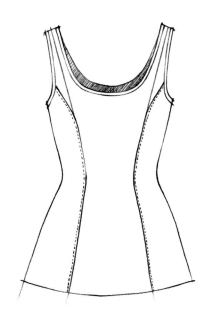

Modified princess seam on Camisole Tank

ALTERING HEMLINES

There are several ways to adjust the length of tops, skirts, and dresses. Depending on the pattern, these different ways may change the shape of the garment. When working with a curved hemline, you can use a curved ruler to help keep a consistent line, or simply trace the curve of the original pattern onto the altered pattern to retain the hem's original shape. Keep in mind that as you shorten or lengthen a garment at the hem, this can also slightly change the shape of the pattern piece. See information on perimeter changes starting on page 93 and internal pattern changes starting on page 96 to determine which method will work best for your particular project.

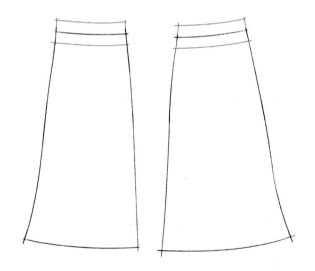

Lengthening or shortening a hem at the skirt's waistline

To alter the length at the perimeter

You can adjust the hem's length at the perimeter of the hem itself, or add or subtract length at the waistline. To lengthen or shorten the hem by 2" (5 cm) or less at the hem itself:

1. Prepare your pattern pieces as outlined on page 90.

2. Determine how much you want to increase or decrease the length of the hemline.

3. Carefully note on the pattern piece(s) to be altered the amount determined in Step 2 to be added to or subtracted from each seam.

4. Mark the actual alteration at each seam to form the new hemline.

5. Using your original pattern as a guide, a straight ruler, and/or pattern curves, draw a smooth line on your traced pattern to form the new hemline.

6. Test your pattern in fabric by making an unembellished basic garment. Note that increasing or decreasing the width of your pattern may affect the fabric yardage needed.

To lengthen or shorten the hem at the perimeter of the waistline, follow all the instructions above, making your alteration at the waist rather than the hem (if the waistline has darts, leave them intact, and make the alteration only on the seam lines). This technique is often used when you want to keep the skirt's same identical sweep and shape but shorten it. Subtracting length from the waistline will generally make the skirt (or garment body) slightly larger in width, and adding to the waistline will generally make the width of the skirt (or garment body) slightly smaller since the lines will angle inward.

Lengthening or shortening a garment at the hemline

We like to stitch a 1" (2.5 cm) border of beads to the hem of our Mid-Length Fitted Skirt (see page 60). We add the beaded border after the skirt is constructed, starting it 1" (2.5 cm) up from the hem and stitching the beads very close together using a single strand of button craft thread (see page 132). The beads give the hem some weight and sparkle. Beaded borders can also be added to necklines, sleeve hems, or any spot on any garment where you want some extra detail.

To alter the length internally

1. For changes of more than 2" (5 cm) or to retain the pattern silhouette and/or hem's sweep, prepare your pattern pieces as outlined on page 90.

2. Determine how much you want to increase or decrease the length.

3. Determine how many pattern pieces you need to alter internally.

4. Draw a horizontal line on each pattern piece (which will usually be perpendicular to the grain line) at the point(s) where you want to increase or decrease the width.

5. Cut the pattern piece partially or fully in half at the horizontal line.

6. To increase the length, add an additional piece of paper behind your two cut pieces, separate them by the amount of the desired increase in length, and tape both cut pieces securely to the backing layer. To reduce the length of the piece, overlap the two cut pieces by the desired decrease in length, and tape the two cut pieces securely into place. Note that in a shaped pattern piece, this method may also alter the perimeter edges at the seam lines. This method can also slightly modify the shape of the pattern piece. Keep these changes in mind as you work with your individual figure since each change will affect how the garment fits you.

7. Review the perimeter of each altered piece to make sure that no adjustments need to be made to smooth the seams.

8. Using your ruler or pattern curves, draw a smooth line from your alteration to re-join the original pattern line on either side of each alteration.

9. Test your pattern in fabric by making an unembellished basic garment. Keep in mind that increasing or decreasing the length of your pattern may affect the fabric yardage needed.

Additional Ways to Alter Length

You can also lengthen or shorten a garment at the high hip, low hip, or both. Additionally, you may want to add or subtract from the length at multiple points across the pattern piece as shown in the illustration below. For example, you may have a longer hip and want to add some length at the hip and an additional amount nearer the hem.

We lengthened the coat at right by slashing the paper pattern piece for the coat nearer the hem and adding stripe across the grain of the garment to increase the finished length. Use this and any pattern alteration as an opportunity for additional design detail. Here we used a brightly colored stripe of fabric to highlight our change and create a color-block effect. See page 52 for details on adding a stripe to increase the final width of a garment.

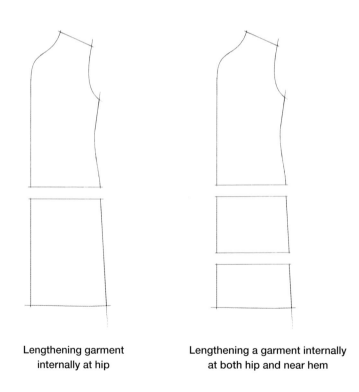

Lengthening garment
internally at hip

Lengthening a garment internally
at both hip and near hem

ALTERING NECKLINES

You can easily raise or lower a neckline by using your curved ruler to help draw a smooth line. Neckline drop (how far a neckline plunges from the shoulder seam) and width vary a lot from style to style, as you can see from the drawings below, and the necklines on all our garment and dress patterns can be modified endlessly.

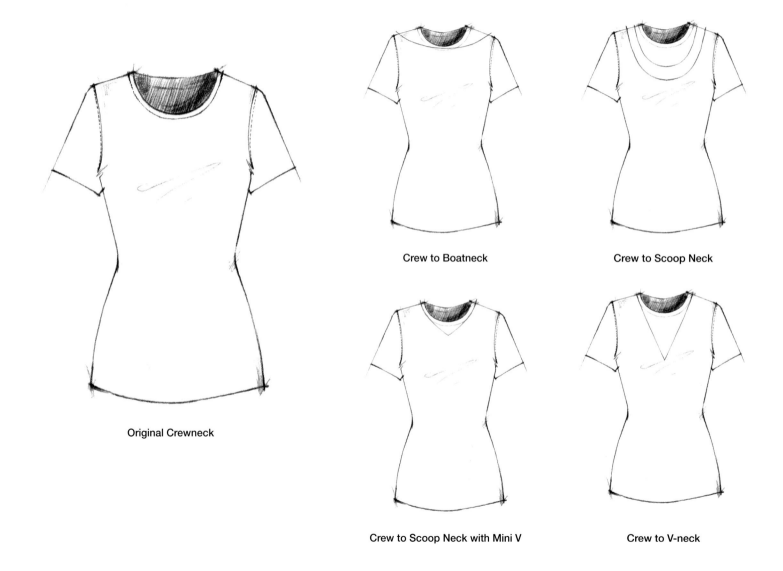

Original Crewneck

Crew to Boatneck

Crew to Scoop Neck

Crew to Scoop Neck with Mini V

Crew to V-neck

To raise or lower a neckline

1. Prepare your pattern pieces as outlined on page 90.

2. Determine how much you want to raise or lower the neckline.

3. Carefully note on your pattern pieces the amounts that you want to add or subtract. Keep in mind that a neckline can be changed by equal amounts around the front and back curve. Alternatively you may want to alter only the drop of the front or the back curve, tapering gradually to nothing as each curve reaches the shoulder.

4. On the pattern, use your French and/or pattern curves to draw a smooth line from the new neckline drop to the shoulder seam, following the desired curve and adding extra paper behind the neckline if you want to raise the front or back neckline.

5. Test your pattern in fabric by making an unembellished basic garment.

Altering garment's entire neckline

Altering only part of neckline, shown here from center front (with no change to back pattern pieces)

To alter a neckline across multiple pattern pieces

When a neckline involves multiple pattern pieces, as in our Corset, Camisole, Tank, and Fitted dresses, you will use a slightly different alteration method:

1. Prepare your pattern pieces as outlined on page 90.

2. Determine how much you want to raise or lower the neckline.

3. If you want to raise the neckline, add pattern paper behind the neckline curve of each pattern piece, and tape it securely into place. If you want to lower the neckline, skip this step.

4. Lay your cut pattern pieces together, making sure to overlap the seam allowances, as shown at top on the facing page, to join the neckline across the pattern pieces.

5. Carefully note each pattern piece to be altered with the amounts that you want to add or subtract. Keep in mind that you can alter a neckline by equal or unequal amounts around its front and back curve.

6. Use your French curve and/or pattern curves to draw a smooth line from the new neckline drop to the shoulder seam following the desired curve.

7. Test your pattern in fabric by making an unembellished basic garment.

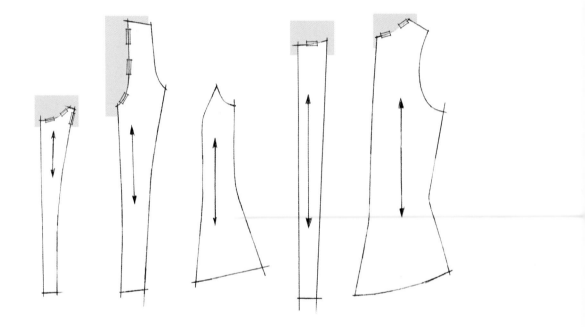

Adding paper behind Corset pattern pieces at neckline to raise neckline

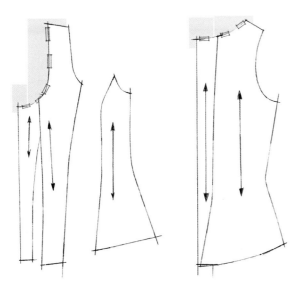

Overlapping Corset pattern pieces to alter neckline

A note on gaping: Low necklines like V-necks or scoop necks can sometimes gape, or fall away from the body, after the garment is sewn. This can happen when the shape and size of the neckline is too large for your body type and also when the cotton-jersey neckline has been stretched during the construction process. To eliminate gaping, adjust the neckline by lifting the bodice at the shoulder to remove excess fabric between the bust and the shoulder, as shown in the illustration below. Be especially careful when handling cut knit pieces since scooped-out areas likes necklines and armholes can get stretched if over-handled, pulled, or strained. Stretching or straining these areas can substantially affect the fit of your garment.

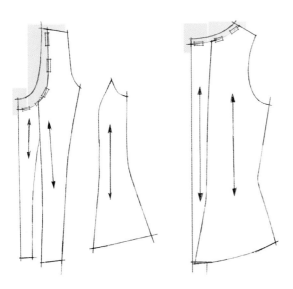

Raising neckline of Corset pattern

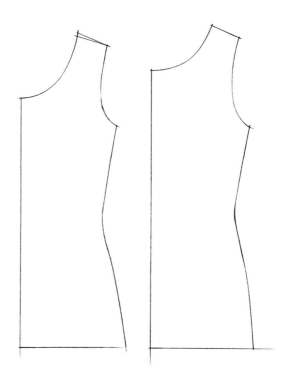

Eliminate gaping at neckline by lifting bodice at shoulder to remove excess fabric between bust and shoulder.

Altering the width of the shoulders and straps

Straps and shoulders can be easily widened or reduced for a perfect fit. To change the width of a strap or shoulder:

1. Prepare your pattern pieces as outlined on page 90.

2. Determine how much you want to change the width.

3. Carefully note on your pattern pieces the amounts that you want to add or subtract. Keep in mind that you can alter a strap shoulder by equal amounts on each side of the strap or shoulder or just on one side, as shown below at right.

4. On the pattern, use your French curve and/or pattern curves to draw a smooth line from the new strap or shoulder width to meet the neckline or armhole and following the desired curve.

5. Test your pattern in fabric by making an unembellished basic garment.

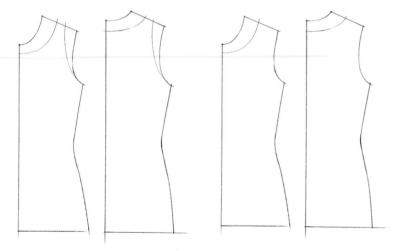

Change on each side of strap   Change on one side of strap

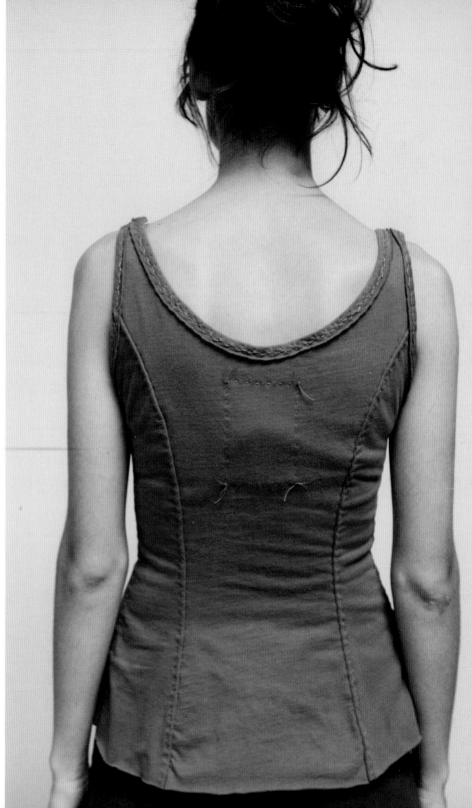

SLEEVE ALTERATIONS

A variety of sleeve shapes and lengths can be made from a single sleeve pattern. Our sleeved garments are marked with a variety of sleeve lengths that are easy to adjust to your individual projects:

Cap sleeve—This very short sleeve generally stops at the edge of the shoulder.

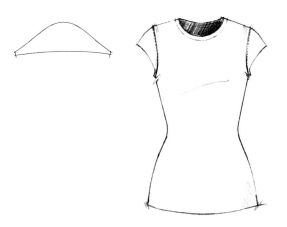

Short sleeve—This sleeve usually stops midway on the upper arm but can be lengthened or shortened to fit each individual body.

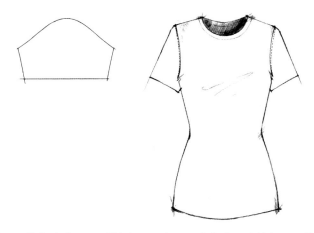

¾ sleeve—Normally stopping midway on the lower arm, this sleeve can be lengthened or shortened to fit each individual body.

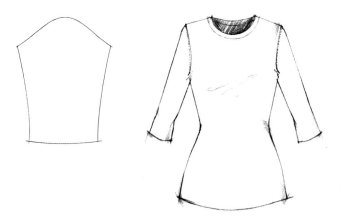

Long fluted sleeve—This is our sleeve of choice at Alabama Chanin since it is fitted enough to make a pretty line but flares slightly at the bottom to provide a wider range of movement at the wrist.

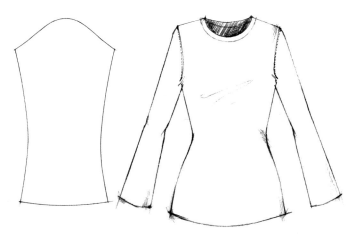

Shaping armholes and sleeve caps requires complicated pattern alterations, but there is a wide variety of sleeve types that you can easily create with very simple paper-pattern alterations to a basic sleeve pattern:

Long fitted sleeve—This sleeve tapers all the way to the wrist and is made by tapering the Fluted Sleeve pattern, as shown below:

Gathered short sleeve—This sleeve has a smooth cap that flares out at the hem, produced by slashing and speading the sleeve hem but not the cap, and then gathering the hem.

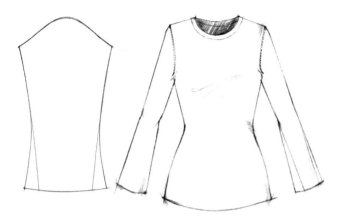

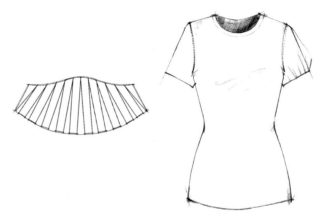

Long gathered sleeve—This loose-fitting sleeve increases to a wide sweep at the hem, which is often gathered to create a billowing effect. This sleeve is created by slashing and spreading the hem but not the sleeve cap.

You can also use the nested pattern to make a smaller or larger armhole opening (see page 88 for more on nested patterns). Note how the sleeve shape and the drop of the point changes with each pattern size.

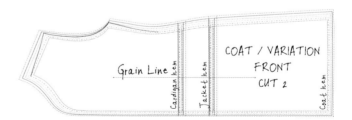

Perimeter vs. internal sleeve alterations

Follow the direction on page 112 for lengthening or shortening a hemline to make simple perimeter changes at the sleeve's hem.

To make internal changes to a sleeve's length, follow the directions on page 114 for lengthening or shortening the hemline.

To increase or reduce the sleeve's width, follow the instructions on page 96 for making internal adjustments, slashing and spreading or overlapping the sleeve pieces to arrive at the desired width.

Note: Avoid working in the sleeve cap since this will change how the sleeve piece attaches to the garment body.

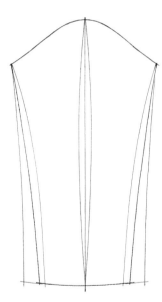

A few possible internal and perimeter changes for a sleeve

Adapting Commercial Patterns to Create Alabama Chanin-Style Garments

While we love it when sewers make projects following our patterns, it is also possible to create Alabama Chanin-style clothing with sewing patterns from other companies and independent pattern designers. We have featured many of these sewing projects on our online journal (www.alabamachanin.com/journal) and continue to update that selection on a regular basis.

This means you can take a pattern written for machine-sewing and/or woven fabrics and adapt it to our hand-stitched cotton-jersey style. Using these sewing patterns allows for an endless array of possibilities with our techniques and embellishment.

We have done a lot of experimenting and have found that most commercial patterns work with our techniques as long as we follow these basic guidelines:

- Embrace experimentation. We have made a lot of beautiful garments following other companies' sewing patterns, but this is not an exact science.

- When choosing a pattern, simply look for something that you really want to wear yourself. You can choose from sewing patterns designed for both knit and woven fabrics. This may be surprising since, traditionally, sewers are directed to follow each pattern specifically, using woven fabrics with patterns created for wovens and knit fabrics with patterns designed for knits.

- Do not choose heavily structured patterns with intricate tailoring that requires heavy interfacing. While these patterns can work with our techniques, they tend to be more difficult to navigate.

- Eliminate linings and interfacing. Because of the weight of our cotton jersey, we have never used an interfacing in the patterns we construct in our style.

- Eliminate zippers. Cotton jersey stretches, and as long as you use a stretch stitch (see page 138) around the neckline, you should be able to get into and out of all garments without a zipper.

- When in question, make an unembellished basic garment sample.

- Reduce all seam allowances to ¼" (6 mm) in order to use our standard Alabama Chanin seams (see page 144). This means cutting down each pattern piece in which a seam allowance is included. This is because the ⅝" (9 mm) seam allowances in most standard patterns produce bulky seams in cotton jersey that detract from the line and fit of the finished garment.

- Remove the seam allowance altogether on necklines and armholes on garments that do not have collars or sleeves, and then bind the edges to finish them (see page 22).

- Eliminate all buttonholes, and use snaps as closures. We have found it time-consuming to make beautiful buttonholes with cotton jersey, which often sag over time and/or become stretched out.

- Choose a pattern that matches your skill level. Some patterns are labeled by the pattern company for advanced sewers—take heed.

- We have never made pants from an existing pattern, but that does not mean it would not work. I love a challenge, so you may see that in our future. Meanwhile, perhaps you will want to try a pair of pants on your own.

- Keep an open mind. Since the pattern you choose may not have been designed for hand-sewing, think about your construction steps in advance in order to try to pinpoint and plan a strategy to resolve any possible areas of difficulty.

ADAPTING A COMMERCIAL PATTERN, STEP-BY-STEP

Below is a basic step-by-step guide for adapting a garment from another pattern company to the Alabama Chanin style.

1. Choose your garment size and cut out the pattern, reducing all seam allowances to ¼" (6 mm) and eliminating seam allowances on necklines without collars and armholes without sleeves.

2. Lay out the cotton-jersey fabric you will be using on your cutting surface single- or double-layer, as described on the pattern instructions, being careful not to pull or stretch the fabric.

3. Cut out your garment following all directions for grain lines and eliminating notches and most facings (evaluate facings on a pattern-by-pattern basis, using facings only where you want to clean-finish an edge; see page 26). In the case of most jackets, you will add a binding to encase the garment's center front edges and/or hems. Alternatively you could clean-finish (see page 26) the front panels before adding any embellishment.

4. Although you will not cut notches, you still need to mark the notches' position from the original pattern with tailor's chalk in order to use these marks as match points or to note other construction points on the pattern.

5. If you are making a double-layer rather than a single-layer garment, repeat the process in Steps 1–4 above, using the first layer that you cut as a pattern guide for cutting the second layer.

6. Add stenciling (optional; see page 146).

7. For a double-layer garment, align and pin the pattern pieces' top and backing layers together, as explained in Step 6 of the A-Line Dress instructions on page 19.

8. Add embellishment (optional; see page 150).

9. Construct the garment using ¼" (6 mm) seam allowances and following all other pattern instructions.

10. Bind the neckline and armholes.

PART 3

BASIC TECHNIQUES + EMBELLISHMENT GLOSSARY

Here we present a basic overview of Alabama Chanin's core sewing and embellishment techniques, which we have spent more than a decade refining. They are the same ones used by our artisans to create extraordinary garments for our retail partners and customers. These techniques are specific to our work with cotton jersey, and we urge you to review them since they vary from often–taught standards.

From the types of threads and needles we use, to the length of our stitches and how we tie our knots, to how we make our stencils, embroider, and apply appliqué, our techniques have come to define our work as a company. We have used them to define how we look at fashion, making, manufacturing, and, on a larger scale, sustainability and community. If you are interested in delving more deeply into the details, you may want to check out our earlier books: *Alabama Stitch Book*, *Alabama Studio Style*, and *Alabama Studio Sewing + Design*.

Supplies

Below are the tools and supplies we most often use as we design and manufacture our collections. We suggest that you build your own supply collection over time as your desires, needs, and skills evolve.

Basic Patternmaking Supplies

Pattern paper (preferably gridded)

Sharp pencil or mechanical pencil with #5 HB lead (see *Note below)

Colored pencils, for marking patterns (optional)

Eraser

Paper scissors

Clear plastic ruler

Curved pattern-making ruler(s)

French curve or any assortment of curved drawing tools

Tape measure

Drawing compass (optional)

Tape calculator (correct calculations are extremely important)

Note: It's very important to make sharp lines when working on intricate patterns since even a 1/16" (2 mm) difference—about the width of a pencil mark—can produce huge pattern changes when multiplied by a garment's many seam allowances (see page 144).

Basic Sewing Supplies

Fabric scissors (we prefer the spring-loaded variety since they reduce hand strain)

Rotary cutter and cutting mat

Tailor's chalk or disappearing-ink fabric pen, for transferring patterns to fabric

Permanent marker, for marking pattern paper

Hand-sewing needles in assorted sizes (#9 sharps, embroidery, or milliners needles work well with cotton-jersey fabric and button craft thread)

Button craft thread (which is thicker than all-purpose sewing thread and ideal for hand-sewing)

All-purpose sewing thread (standard lightweight thread designed for use with sewing machines)

Pins (long, thin pins often called "glass head")

Thimble

Small rubber finger cap (for gripping needles)

Needle-nose pliers (for pulling needles through many layers of fabric)

Pincushion

Pattern weights

Seam ripper

Additional Embroidery Supplies (optional)

Embroidery scissors (use a 5" [12 cm] knife-edge for trimming fabric and clipping threads, and 4" [10 cm] embroidery scissors for small, detailed work)

Embroidery floss (a decorative but weak thread for embellishing fabric; normally contains six tightly twisted strands of fine thread)

Cotton yarn and perle cotton (soft cotton knitting yarn), for embroidery

Cotton tape (5 mm), for ribbon embroidery (most often used in our Climbing Daisy embroidery technique)

Cotton-jersey pulls, or ropes (created by cutting cotton jersey into strips and pulling them to make them roll and form "ropes")

Beads (usually glass and large enough to accommodate thick button craft thread), for embellishing garments

Beading needles (long with an eye small enough to pass through beads but large enough to accept thick button craft thread)

Sequins (small metal or plastic disks), for embellishing garments

Basic Stenciling Supplies

Medium- or heavyweight transparent film (preferably Mylar), for making stencils

Acrylic pennant felt, for making stencils

Spray adhesive, for holding stencil in place while painting it

Permanent or textile markers, for transferring stencil designs to fabric

Textile paint, for transferring stencil designs to fabric (we use Createx Airbrush Paint)

Clean spray bottles with adjustable nozzles, for spraying textile paint through stencils onto fabric

Brushes or sponges, for transferring textile paint onto fabric

Airbrush gun and air compressor (recommended only if/when you become very serious about spray-painting stencil designs onto fabric and other surfaces; we use both at the studio)

Butcher paper or scrap fabric, for masking off areas that do not require stenciling

Craft knife

Fold-Over Elastic

We use this stretchable grosgrain elastic binding on the waistbands of all our pull-on skirts. We apply it with a single strand of button craft thread, using a stretch stitch of choice (see page 138) or whipstitch (see page 139). This elastic is about ⅞" (2 cm) wide (before folding), has a central ridge that makes it easy to fold over to encase the fabric edge, and is thin enough to stitch through. We recommend basting (see page 136), not pinning, the fold-over elastic in place with an all-purpose thread before sewing it down permanently to ensure a smooth finish. Not only does pinning such a small strip risk making the layers buckle and causing the finished seam to ripple, but also the pins can be hard to maneuver around when stitching the elastic permanently in place. If you follow all these directions and still have trouble getting your fold-over elastic to behave, try changing your needle size or using a fresh, very sharp needle. Fold-over elastic can be difficult to find, so we have made it available from our online store at www.alabamachanin.com.

Alabama Chanin Cotton-Jersey Fabric

Over the years, we have tried many types and combinations of fabrics for our designs, but we always return to our 100-percent organic cotton jersey. Our artisans, DIY makers, and customers all tell us that it is among the softest and most durable fabrics they have ever worked with or worn. And, amazingly, it softens and becomes more comfortable with each wearing.

Cotton-jersey fabric comes in a variety of weights commonly described as ounces per linear yard. For a decade we used either recycled T-shirts (as described in *Alabama Stitch Book*) and/or a medium-weight jersey that averages 9.80 ounces per linear yard. This medium-weight jersey was introduced in *Alabama Studio Style* and has been the core of our hand-sewn collection since then.

Since the introduction of cotton jersey by the yard, we have worked closely with each producer and supplier to make sure that our fabric meets our strict guidelines for quality and sustainability. Our medium-weight cotton jersey fiber is most often grown in Texas and then sent to North Carolina to be spun, knit into jersey fabric, and dyed. It is then shipped to our studio for production. While this may seem like a lot of moving around, this is considered an extremely local supply chain in our global economy.

In 2010 we added a lightweight jersey to our collections. This fabric, which averages about 5.6 ounces per linear yard, has more drape and a more fluid quality than our medium-weight cotton jersey, and it is transparent in lighter colors. To manufacture the lightweight cotton jersey, it is necessary to begin with cotton with a longer staple (fiber) length than required for the medium-weight jersey, and spinning that fiber requires machinery that is not currently available in the United States. For this reason, we import fine, organic yarn from overseas, then have it knit into our lightweight cotton jersey fabric in North Carolina. When stitching a garment with a single-layer of the lightweight cotton jersey, we sometimes thread our needle with a single strand of our strong button craft thread (see page 132) instead of a double strand, which is our standard in most other cases. I urge you to experiment with the weights in single and double layer and by combining them. Adding embroidery and embellishments further changes and enhances the weight and how the fabrics behave in final garment form. I play with these elements every day and they provide me with endless design inspiration.

Thread, Stitch, and Knotting Basics

BUTTON CRAFT THREAD

This thread is thicker than ordinary sewing thread, and we use it for most of our hand-sewing needs. Made with a polyester core surrounded by very finely spun cotton yarn, is one of the strongest threads we have found.

ALL-PURPOSE THREAD

Designed for use with sewing machines, this standard, lightweight thread is our choice for hand-basting necklines and armholes before constructing garments to keep these curved edges from stretching during construction and for the ruffling techniques described on page 34. We never use this thin thread for embroidery, embellishment, or constructing a garment: Seams and embellishments sewn with all-purpose thread will break, and beads will fall off after wearing and washing a garment only a few times.

EMBROIDERY FLOSS

Embroidery floss is perfect for small, intricate embellishments and where color variation is desired. The floss itself is composed of six loosely twisted strands. We normally use four strands for embroidery (by threading two strands through the needle and doubling them over). We never use this floss for sewing seams since it is not strong enough for this purpose.

STITCH LENGTH AND TENSION

For most projects at Alabama Chanin, we use a double length of button craft thread and make stitches that are between ⅛" (3 mm) and ¼" (6 mm) long; for basting, we use an all-purpose sewing thread and a longer stitch, as explained on page 136. Stitches that are too small will pull through the tiny loops of yarn that make up the cotton-jersey fabric (see the photo on page 135), while stitches that are too big will break more easily or snag as you go about your daily life. Aim not only for uniform stitches and spaces between them but also for even sewing tension. If your sewing tension is too tight, you will pull the seam too tight as you sew, and it will start to gather up. Conversely, if your tension is too loose, your seam will buckle.

THREADING YOUR NEEDLE OR, REALLY, NEEDLING YOUR THREAD

Needling your thread (rather than threading your needle) may sound strange, but it makes perfect sense in that the thread is weaker than the needle and easily moves or bends. Moving the more stable element—the needle—over the thread to "needle the thread" makes this a simple task.

While it is tempting to work with a long length of thread to avoid having to rethread your needle, it is actually better to start with a length of thread that is about the same as the distance between your fingertips to your elbow when doubled. There are several reasons for this: First, a longer thread is more prone to knotting as you sew. Second, if you use an extremely long thread, you will spend more time pulling the thread through your fabric than actually sewing. Third, and most important, as you sew, the thread is being abraded with every stitch you take, and naturally the thread closest to the needle experiences the most abrasion since it is pulled through the fabric more often than the thread closest to the knotted end. Because of this abrasion, the thread closest to the needle becomes weaker and weaker as you sew and sometimes breaks. When threading a needle, we recommend measuring from your elbow to your fingertips, doubling it (assuming you're sewing with a doubled thread), then adding a few inches to accommodate your knots.

"LOVING YOUR THREAD"

When thread is made, microscopic, curly cotton fibers are twisted tightly into two strands and then twisted together again in a process called "plying." This process produces excess tension on the plied strands that can cause the thread to tangle and knot during hand-sewing. To counter this, we have sorted out a way of reducing this tension that we call "loving your thread."

To "love your thread," cut your thread to the length desired (see above), and pull the thread through the needle until the two ends are the same length. Hold the doubled thread between your thumb and index finger, and run your fingers along it from the needle to the end of the loose tails. Repeat this several times or until your thread—and your mind—feel relaxed. What you are doing is working the tension out of the highly twisted thread by rubbing, pressure, and the natural oils on your fingers and training those two lengths of thread to lie side-by-side. After a good loving, you are ready to knot your thread and start sewing.

KNOTTING OFF

In hand-sewing, the knot in your thread anchors and holds your entire seam. Since cotton jersey is a knit fabric made by continuously looping a thin yarn through itself to form a knitted "web," very small holes are formed where the yarn loops. If you knot your sewing thread with a small knot, that knot can pull through any of the small holes in the fabric's structure. When the thread pulls through the fabric, the thin yarn is often broken causing the fabric to "run" and produce an even bigger hole. Therefore, for most projects, we recommend a double strand of thread and a large double knot to anchor it, as shown below.

Additionally we leave ½"- (12-mm-) long thread tails after tying off all of our knots since wearing and washing your garment will cause these thread tails to shorten over time. When we start with long tails, we know the garment will maintain its original integrity from the first day it was created. We often say that we leave the tails long since our garments are being sewn "for this generation, and the next, and the next."

One important design decision we make when starting any project is how to handle the knots. There are three options: knots that show on the project's right side (outside), knots that show on the wrong side (inside), or a combination of the two.

Tying a Double Knot

To tie a double knot, after bringing the needle up through the fabric, make a thread loop, then pull the needle through the loop, using your forefinger or thumb to nudge the knot into place, flush with the fabric. Then repeat the process to make a double knot. After making a second knot, cut the thread, leaving a ½" (12 mm) tail.

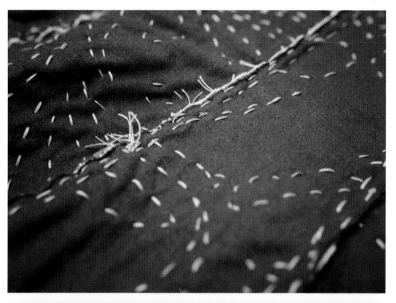

Top to bottom: Knots on wrong side, knots on right side

Cutting Out a Pattern

Cutting out the pattern is an important step that requires precision since it will be the foundation of your garment or project. Below are instructions for cutting out a pattern using cotton-jersey fabric.

SUPPLIES

Printed project pattern

Cotton-jersey fabric

Tailor's chalk or disappearing-ink fabric pen

Paper scissors

Garment scissors

1. Choose Size and Cut Out Pattern

The garment patterns on the CD at the end of this book provide five sizes (from XS to XL) in which the garment can be made. Decide which size garment you want to make (see page 80 and also the sidebar "Mixing and Matching Pattern Sizes" on page 88), make any alterations or corrections (see Part 2), and use your paper scissors to cut out the pattern in your desired size and with any changes or adaptations.

2. Prepare Fabric for Cutting and Stitching

It is important to prevent the cotton-jersey fabric from stretching as you cut and work with it. To avoid misshapen fabric when laying it out on your work surface, do not stretch it or smooth it out by pulling on it; instead lightly pat the cotton jersey into place with your fingertips. The directions for each project or garment will tell you whether to lay out and cut your fabric single- or double-layer. If you need to lay out your fabric double-layer—or if you want to add a backing layer behind the top fabric layer to make a heavier garment or provide support for a lot of embellishment—fold the fabric's width either with or across the grain (see the discussion of grain on the facing page; the project directions will tell you which way to fold the fabric) with wrong sides together and the edges aligned.

3. Transfer Pattern to Fabric

Lay your paper pattern pieces on top of your fabric, making sure that the pattern's marked grain line runs in the same direction as the fabric's grain line (see facing page). This is important because, when cutting out a garment, you want the grain line on the cut fabric to run vertically from the neckline to waistline, so the fabric can stretch around your body.

Trace around your pattern piece with tailor's chalk or a disappearing-ink fabric pen, holding the pattern in place with the palm of your hand or with pattern weights (or even canned goods). We prefer holding or weighting the pattern to pinning it on the fabric, which, in the case of cotton jersey, often skews the fabric and makes the cutting uneven. We have also found that this holding/weighting strategy prevents nicking and tearing the pattern, which often results from pinning it in place.

Since many garments have more than one pattern piece, we suggest cutting out all the pieces of a garment at once. Laying out all the pattern pieces together on your fabric before you start cutting enables you to figure out how to place the pieces to use your fabric most efficiently.

4. Cut Pattern from Fabric

Using fabric scissors, cut out the pattern pieces as called for in your project directions, trying your best to cut just inside the chalked or penned line you traced around the pattern. By cutting away all of the visible chalk or ink (but not cutting beyond the marked line), you will help ensure a perfect fit.

Cutting Cotton Jersey

If you look closely at cotton jersey's right side, you'll see straight vertical columns of stitches that make up the grain line. On cotton jersey's wrong side, you'll see a series of little loops. To cut the fabric with the grain, align your scissors or rotary cutter with the fabric's grain, that is, with its vertical columns of stitches. Likewise, to fold the fabric with the grain, fold it along the vertical column of stitches, and to fold it across the grain, fold it across the stitch columns. Working with the correct grain line enhances a finished garment's stretchability at key points (for example, at the armholes, across the bust, and at other parts of the body where we need a bit of stretch). See also the discussion on page 91 of reestablishing the grain line on an altered pattern.

Right side

Wrong side

Our Core Stitches

We use three categories of stitches in our work at Alabama Chanin: stitches that do not stretch, for construction, reverse appliqué, and other embellishments; stitches that do stretch, for sewing necklines, armholes, and other areas in a project that requires give; and stitches that are purely decorative for embellishment.

NON-STRETCH STITCHES

When working with all but one of our non-stretch stitches—the blanket stitch—you will move the needle in a continuous straight line. In the case of the blanket stitch, you will use a looping technique to create a straight line.

Straight, or Running, Stitch

Bring needle up at A, go back down at B, and come up at C, making stitches and spaces between them the same length (about ⅛"–¼" [3–6 mm] long).

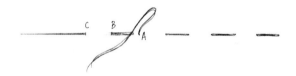

Basting Stitch

This stitch is a longer, looser variation of the straight, or running, stitch, and involves simply making both stitches and spaces between them about ½" (12 mm) long.

Backstitch

Bring needle up at A, go back down at B, and come up at C. Then insert needle just ahead of B, and come up at D. Next insert needle just ahead of C, and come up at E. Continue this overall pattern.

Blanket Stitch

Bring needle up at A, and hold thread with finger to left of A. Insert needle at B, about ¼" (6 mm) below and to left of A. Come back up at C, directly above B, making sure needle stitches over, not under, thread. Pull up thread so it lies tightly against thread at C, and repeat process. Continue working stitch, keeping its length and spacing consistent, to complete entire edge or eyelet.

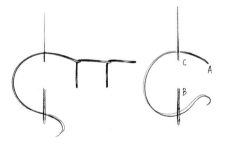

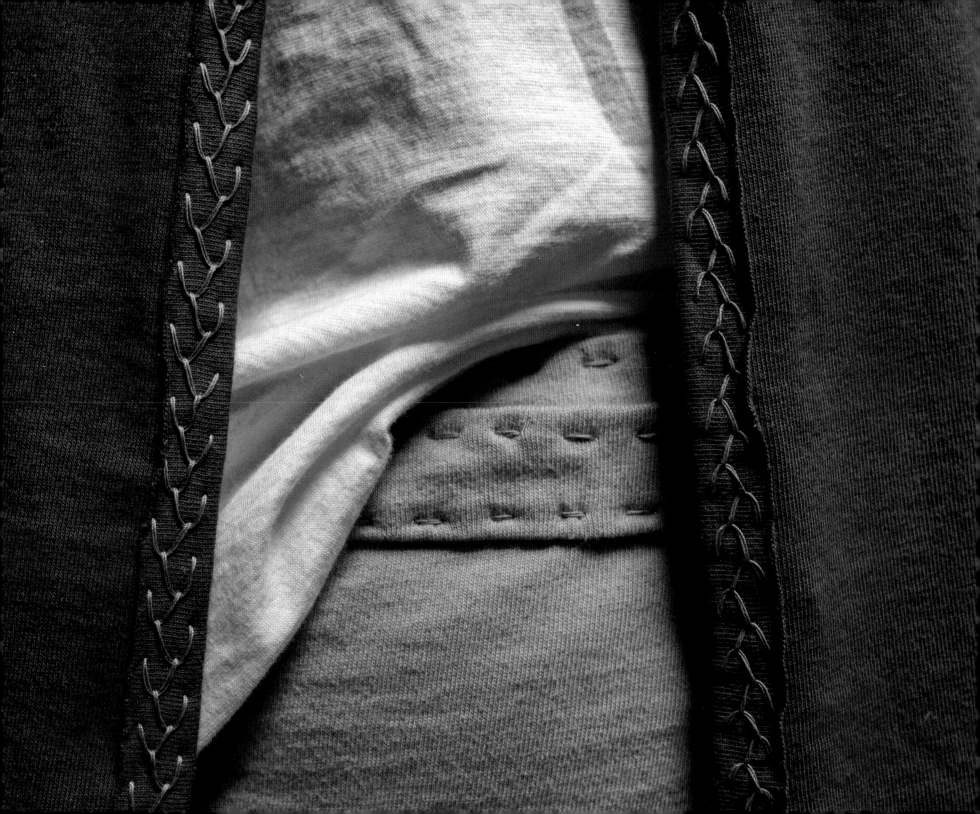

STRETCH/DECORATIVE STITCHES

When sewing a stretch stitch, you will move the needle at an angle, producing stitching lines that are broken into diagonal or other nonlinear segments, which allow the knit fabric to retain its stretch. It is important to choose a stretch stitch when working a neckline or another area of a garment that needs to be flexible. Of course, stretch stitches can also be used for purely decorative purposes. Adding beads to each stitch increases the impact. Choose a needle that will allow the threaded needle to pass through the bead and base the number of beads you pick up on the desired effect. For more information about beading, see page 160.

Herringbone Stitch

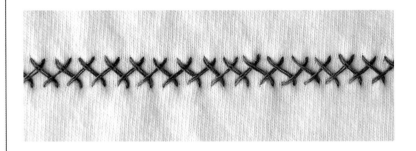

Bring needle up at A, go back down at B, come up at C, and go down at D to complete one herringbone stitch. To start next stitch, come back up at new point A, go back down at new point B, and continue working in above pattern to create a row of herringbone stitches, keeping their length and spacing consistent.

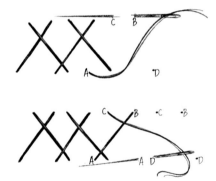

Featherstitch

This stitch is worked along four imaginary parallel vertical lines. Bring needle up at A, go back down at B, and come up at C, moving needle over thread to make open loop. Repeat process on other side, working downward, and continue to alternate sides until you have completed a row.

Parallel Whipstitch

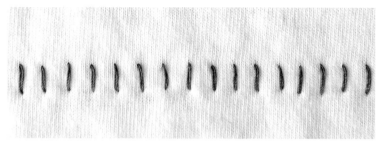

Bring needle up at A, go back down at B, and come up at C, making both stitches and spaces between them ⅜" (1 cm).

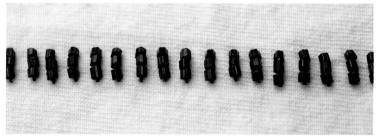

Rosebud Stitch

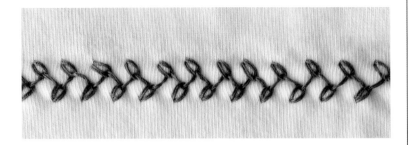

Work this stitch along two imaginary parallel lines, starting by bringing needle up at A. Loop thread above and to right of A, and insert needle back down at B, just to left of A. Bring needle back up at C, pulling thread over, not under, thread loop you made. Go back down at D, and come back up at E. Loop thread below and to right of E, go back down at F, and come up G, pulling thread over, not under, thread loop. Continue repeating stitch pattern, alternating back and forth between parallel lines.

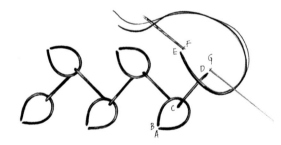

Chevron Stitch

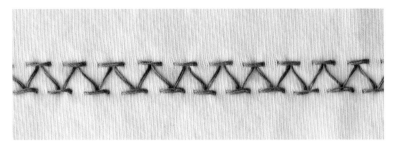

Work stitch along two imaginary parallel lines. Start by bringing needle up at A, go back down at B, and emerge at C. Then insert needle at D, and come back up at E. To form top of chevron stitch, go back down at F, and come up at G. Then move back to imaginary bottom line, and continue working stitch, as before, alternating between top and bottom lines.

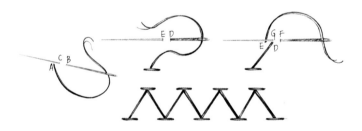

Snail Trail Stitch

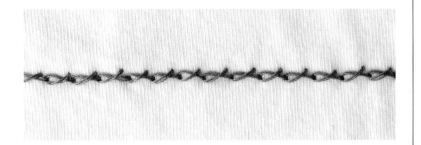

Work stitch along imaginary line, bringing needle up at A, making loop, and going back down at B. Come back up at C, through loop and over thread to secure loop in place.

Zigzag Chain Stitch

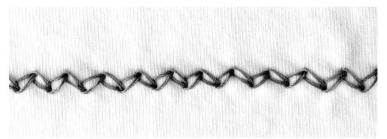

Note that this decorative Zigzag Chain Stitch can also be worked in a straight line as a simple chain stitch. Bring needle up at A, form thread loop, and go back down at B (very close to A, but not in it). Come back up at C, placing needle's point over thread and pulling thread through. To form next loop, insert needle at D, just inside the first loop to keep it in place, bring needle up at E, placing needle's point over thread, and pull thread through. Continue working this pattern, alternating from side to side.

Cretan Stitch

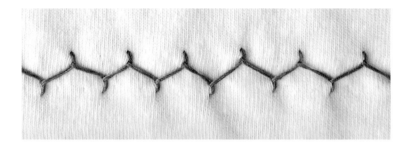

Bring needle up at A, go down at B, and come back up at C, making a downward vertical stitch while bringing needle over thread. Insert needle again at D, and come back up at E, making an upward vertical stitch while bringing needle over thread. Continue to repeat stitch pattern.

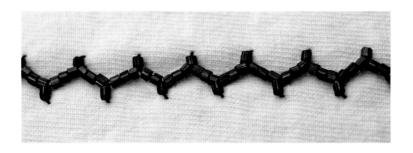

Cross-Stitch

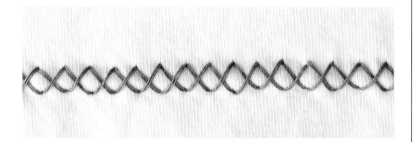

Bring needle up at A, go back down at B, and come up at C; continue this pattern to end of row. Then work same stitch in opposite direction, from lower right to upper left over previous stitches, to form an X.

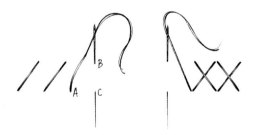

Double Cretan Stitch

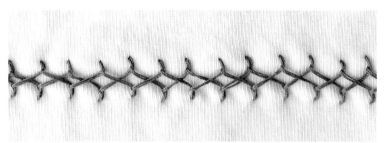

To create the Double Cretan Stitch, we work the Cretan Stitch from page 139 twice across the same line: Simply work your first row of Cretan Stitch across your project as required, and then work a second Cretan Stitch on top of the first row, in a mirror image of your first row to create an interesting diamond shape in the middle. You may also choose to vary the widths of your two Cretan stitches and the color of threads to achieve a variety of stunning results.

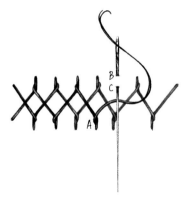

We never work beads into Double Cretan Stitch as we find it too difficult.

Seams

For each garment at Alabama Chanin, we decide whether to expose the seams on the outside of the garment or to hide the seams on the inside of the garment, creating our terms "outside" or "inside" seams. After creating an outside or inside seam you may also choose to leave that seam as is, creating what we call a "floating" seam, or you may choose to sew that seam allowance down to the garment to create a "felled" seam. When the seam allowances are exposed on the garment's right side, or outside, they tend to highlight the garment's structure. Conversely, when the seam allowances are hidden inside the garment on the wrong side, the look of the garment is more streamlined. (See also "Clean-Finishing Seams" on page 26.) At Alabama Chanin, we most often employ Outside Floating, Outside Felled, and Inside Felled seams. We often avoid Inside Floating seams as the extra fabric left floating inside a garment can add the appearance of extra bulk on the body—which most women don't want.

Wrap-Stitching Seams

To anchor your seam and ensure that it stays flat with no hint of gathering or pulling, begin and end it by wrap-stitching the fabric's raw edges. To do this, wrap a loop of thread around the edge of the fabric at the first and last stitches, as shown in the illustration below.

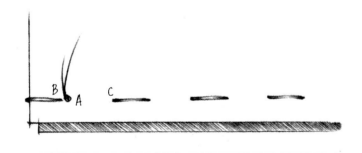

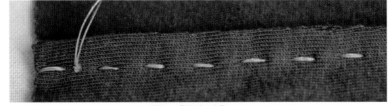

Wrap-Stitched Seam

FLOATING SEAMS

When using floating seams in a garment, it is important to make sure that every seam floats, even when one seam intersects another seam. To stitch a floating seam that intersects another floating seam, stitch under the sewn seam being intersected so that its seam allowances continue to float, and then continue stitching the new seam as usual on the other side of the intersected seam.

Floating Seam on Right Side

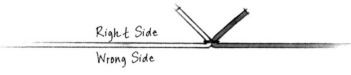

Outside Floating Seam

To make a floating seam that shows on the right side of a garment, pin the two cut fabric pieces being seamed with wrong sides together; then stitch the seam on the fabric's right side. The resulting seam will be visible on the project's right side, or outside.

Floating Seam on Wrong Side

Inside Floating Seam

To make a floating seam that is hidden on the wrong side, or inside, of a garment, pin the two cut fabric pieces being seamed with right sides together; then stitch the seam on the fabric's wrong side. The resulting seam will be only visible on the project's wrong side.

FELLED SEAMS

To decide which direction to fold and fell your seams, start at the garment's center front or center back, and always fell seams toward the side of your body. As a general rule, fell side seams toward the garment's back.

Felled Seam on the Right Side

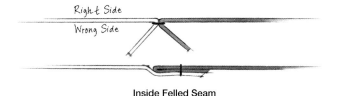

Outside Felled Seam

To sew a felled seam on the garment's right side, first sew a floating seam on the right side. Then fold over the finished seam's allowances together to one side, and stitch them down on the project's right side with a parallel row of stitches ⅛" (3 mm) from the allowances' cut edges, or down the center of the allowances. This seam will be visible on the garment's right side.

Felled Seam on the Wrong Side

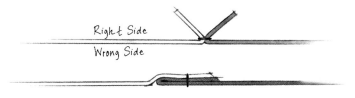

Inside Felled Seam

To sew a felled seam on the garment's wrong side, first sew a floating seam on the wrong side. Then fold over the finished seam's allowances together to one side, and stitch them down on the project's wrong side with a parallel row of stitches ⅛" (3 mm) from the allowances' cut edges, or down the center of the allowances. This seam will be visible on the garment's wrong side.

Open-Felled Seam

You can also open-fell your seam on the right or wrong side by stitching down each seam allowance with a decorative stitch.

Inside Floating Seam

Inside Felled Seam

Outside Floating Seam

Outside Felled Seam

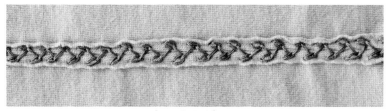

Open-Felled Seam

Stenciling

We use stencils as tools to transfer decorative patterns onto projects and garments. The stenciled patterns are used as guides for positioning embroidery and beading on many of our projects. On pages 149 and 155–159 and on this book's CD are the Magdalena, Polka Dot, and New Leaves stencils featured on garments in this book. You can find additional stencils in our other books (as well as information on making your own stencil) and on our website. A wide variety of ready-to-use stencils is also sold at many craft and sewing stores.

SINGLE, REPEATING, AND ALLOVER STENCIL DESIGNS

Once you have chosen a stencil pattern and/or created a ready-to-use stencil, you will need to decide where to place the stencil design on your cut pieces of fabric. For some projects, you might want to transfer a single repeat or double repeat of the stencil. For others you might want to repeat the stencil to cover the garment fabric allover. If you are working with a relatively small piece of fabric and a large stencil, that single stencil may produce an allover pattern. If you are working with a large piece of fabric and a small stencil, then you will have to either transfer your stencil design multiple times or make your own larger stencil. Follow the instructions for transferring a stencil to fabric on page 148.

A-Line Dress with New Leaves stencil pattern placed only at neckline and hem

A-Line Dress with New Leaves stencil pattern allover

HOW TO TRANSFER A STENCIL DESIGN

We like to transfer stencil designs to fabric by spray-painting through our stencils. Spray-painting can be done with either a spray bottle or an airbrush gun. Using a spray bottle is a great way to get started transferring designs. If you decide to do multiple projects, you may want to try using an airbrush gun, which is quicker and can be used repeatedly with different colors and paint mixtures. Some paints require heat to set, or become permanent, while others simply need to be air-dried. Whatever method you choose for applying paint, always test your paint on a scrap of fabric before beginning an actual project, and closely follow all the paint supplier's instructions for safety and/ or heat-setting.

If you want to apply paint with a spray bottle, use a clean, recycled bottle or a new one with a manually adjustable nozzle. Before transferring a stencil to your project fabric, play with various mixtures of paint and water to get the effect that you are looking for (the more water you use, the more transparent the color will be).

If you want to apply paint with an airbrush gun, we recommend choosing the most basic, least expensive hobby airbrush with a simple air compressor from your local hardware store. For years, we have used a 6-gallon (23-L), 150-PSI (pounds per square inch) electric air compressor. Play with the PSI on your compressor to find the perfect setting. This can take some time and concentration to sort out, but once you have adjusted your settings, the airbrush should be easy to use and run smoothly for many years. Each time you finish using an airbrush gun, wash and dry it thoroughly so it does not get clogged with dry paint. Store the paint in airtight containers for up to three months; over time small particles that can clog your airbrush form in the paint.

SUPPLIES

Stencil

Cotton-jersey fabric

Textile paint

Spray bottle or airbrush gun

Spray adhesive

1. Prepare Work Surface and Stencil

Cover your work surface with a sheet, towel, or large scrap of fabric to protect it and to keep your garment fabric in place when you're transferring the stencil design. Lay your garment fabric, right side up, on top of the covered work surface.

Apply a light coating of spray adhesive to the back of the stencil, then place it, adhesive side down, on the fabric in the desired position.

2. Transfer Stencil Design

Use a spray bottle or airbrush gun to carefully transfer the stencil onto the fabric by spraying paint inside each of the stencil's cut-out shapes. When you have finished spray-painting the entire stencil, carefully remove the stencil and let the paint dry to the touch.

After the paint has dried, if you want to repeat the stencil design or create an allover design on the fabric, reposition the stencil adjacent to the first stenciled motif, and spray-paint the stencil again. Then let the paint dry to the touch, and repeat this process until you have created the desired design.

3. Dry and Heat-Set, If Required

Finish your stenciled design by letting it dry completely. We normally allow 24 hours for our textile paint (which does not require heat-setting) to air-dry before beginning any additional embellishment or sewing. If you are working with paints that require heat-setting to become permanent, always follow the manufacturer's directions in order to prevent the transferred color from washing out. Also note that if you are working with paints that air-dry, we do not recommend washing the stenciled fabric for a minimum of three weeks so that the paint can cure completely (this does not apply to heat-set paints).

New Leaves

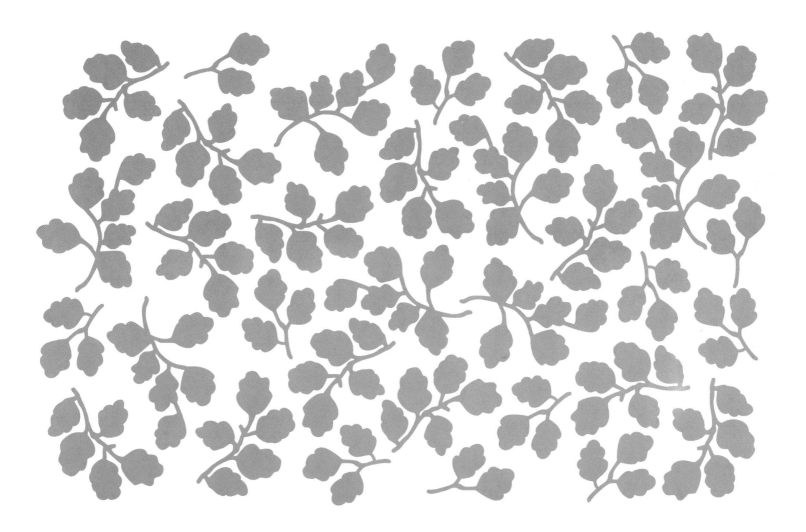

To create the projects in this book, New Leaves was enlarged 500-percent. This artwork can be photocopied and enlarged from this page, or it can be downloaded full-size from this book's CD or from www.alabamachanin.com.

Reverse Appliqué

Reverse appliqué is worked on two layers of fabric: The top layer is stenciled (see page 146) and then stitched to the backing layer; next, part of the top layer is cut away to reveal the backing fabric underneath. We usually do this with a straight stitch (see page 136) and button craft thread or a backstitch (see page 136) and embroidery floss. The backstitch method takes a lot longer to complete.

SUPPLIES

Stencil

Cotton-jersey fabric, for top layer

Cotton-jersey fabric, for backing layer

Textile paint

Button craft thread or embroidery floss

Stencil-transfer tools of choice from page 148

Basic hand-sewing tools from page 128

1. Transfer Stencil Design
Following the instruction on page 146, transfer the stencil design onto the right side of your top-layer fabric, and let the fabric dry thoroughly.

2. Pin Together Top-Layer and Backing Fabrics
Place the cut backing fabric, right side up, behind the area of the top-layer fabric to be appliquéd, also positioned right side up, making sure that the grain lines (see page 135) of both fabrics run in the same direction. Pin the two fabrics together securely.

3. Stitch Outline of Stenciled Shapes
Stitch the two layers of fabric together along the edge of each stenciled shape, using your stitch of choice (see page 136). Be sure to "love your thread" and use a double knot (see pages 132–133) at the beginning and end of each stenciled shape. Continue to move from one shape to the next, stitching around each one and always tying off with a double knot after completing each shape.

4. Trim Top Layer of Fabric Inside Stitched Shapes
Insert the tip of your embroidery scissors into the center of one of the stitched shapes, being careful to puncture only the top layer of fabric. Carefully trim away the inside of the shape, cutting about ⅛" (3 mm) from your stitched outline. This remaining ⅛" (3 mm) is wide enough to prevent the fabric and stitching from raveling, and narrow enough to display the reverse appliqué pattern nicely (along with a sliver of the original stenciled design's paint color). Never cut closer than ⅛" (3 mm) to any stitched outline.

After trimming the top layer of fabric on every shape desired—very small elements in the stenciled design may be too small to trim, so leave them uncut—you have two options for finishing the backing fabric: Either leave the backing fabric as is; or, turn the project wrong side out, and trim away the backing fabric around each stitched shape, leaving a ⅛" (3 mm) border outside the stitched outline. Use extreme caution when using the second method to avoid making holes in your fabric by cutting in the wrong place.

Negative Reverse Appliqué

Negative reverse appliqué looks like appliqué but is worked as reverse appliqué: After stenciling your top-layer fabric and placing it on top of your backing fabric, with both fabrics right side up, straight-stitch ⅛" (3 mm) inside the edge of the stenciled shape; then cut the top layer of fabric ⅛" (3 mm) outside the edge of the stenciled shape, leaving a ¼" (6 mm) sliver of top-layer fabric beyond your stitching line.

Left to right:
Backstitch Reverse Appliqué,
Backstitch Negative Reverse Appliqué

Appliqué

Appliqué is simply a way of applying one fabric on top of another fabric. At Alabama Chanin, we use appliqué to add color, texture, and dimension to our work. Appliqués can be stitched to the base fabric with a variety of stitches, both simple and decorative, producing stunning effects. We generally use a stencil to transfer a design to both the base fabric and appliqué fabric, but you can also draw or paint and cut freehand any shape you want to appliqué.

SUPPLIES

Stencil

Cotton-jersey fabric, for top layer

Cotton-jersey fabric, for appliqué pieces

Textile paint

Stencil-transfer tools of choice from page 148

Basic hand-sewing tools from page 128

1. Stencil Pattern on Base Fabric
Stencil (see page 148) a pattern on the right side of your base fabric where you want to attach the appliqué pieces, remove the stencil, and let the fabric and stencil dry thoroughly.

2. Cut Out Appliqué Pieces
To make your appliqué pieces, flip the dried stencil used in Step 1 to the wrong side, and transfer the stencil pattern to the wrong side (back) of the appliqué fabric. After letting the stenciled fabric dry, begin by cutting out one stenciled shape, 1/16" (2 mm) beyond the outside of the stenciled edge. Once you cut out the shape, flip it over, right side up, and pin it to the corresponding shape in the stenciled pattern on the base fabric. It is important to match up each shape as you cut it—pre-cut pieces can get mixed up, and it is difficult to determine which shape fits where, creating a jigsaw puzzle of stenciled shapes. Repeat for your entire stenciled design by cutting one piece at a time and pinning it into place.

3. Stitch Appliqué Pieces to Project
After positioning each cut appliqué shape, right side up, on top of the corresponding shape in the stenciled design on the base fabric, align the edges of the appliqué and stenciled shapes, and pin the appliqué securely in place. Then attach the appliqué's raw cut edges, using parallel whipstitch or your stitch of choice (see page 138) and a single strand of button craft thread.

Magdalena Stencil

To create the projects in this book, Magdalena was enlarged 440-percent. This artwork can be photocopied and enlarged from this page, or it can be downloaded full-size from this book's CD or from www.alabamachanin.com.

Medium Polka Dot Stencil

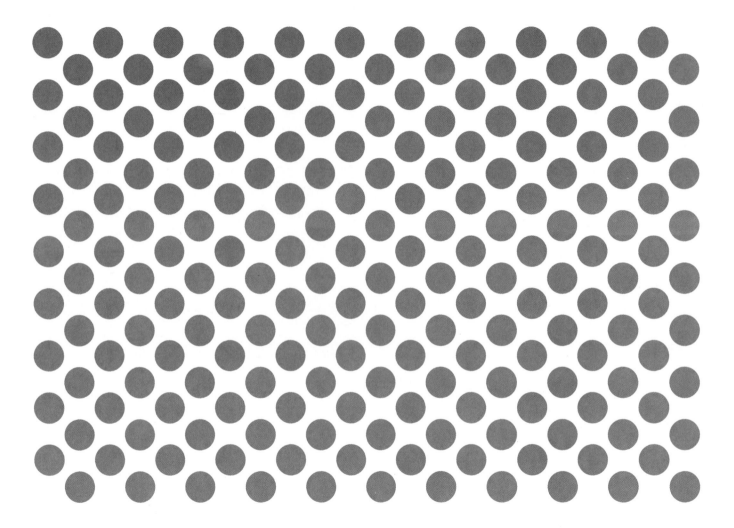

To create the projects in this book, Medium Polka Dot was enlarged 530-percent. This artwork can be photocopied and enlarged from this page, or it can be downloaded full-size from this book's CD or from www.alabamachanin.com.

Small Polka Dot Stencil

To create the projects in this book, Small Polka Dot was enlarged 670-percent. This artwork can be photocopied and enlarged from this page, or it can be downloaded full-size from this book's CD or from www.alabamachanin.com.

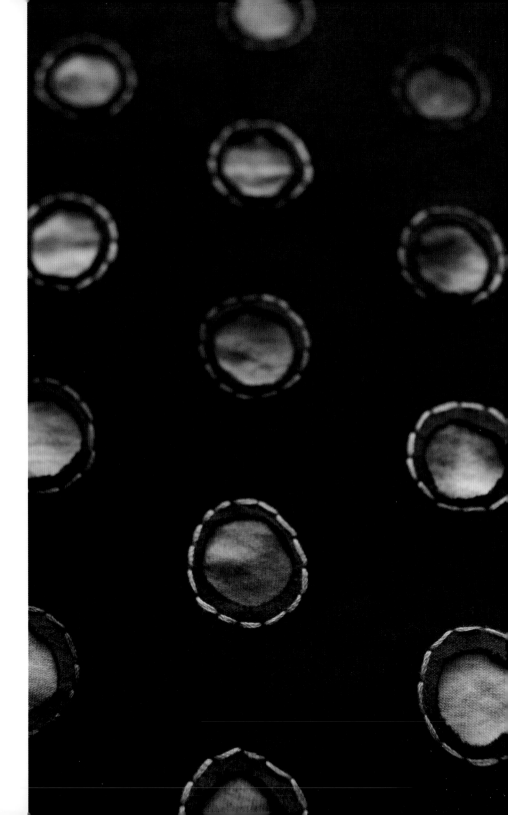

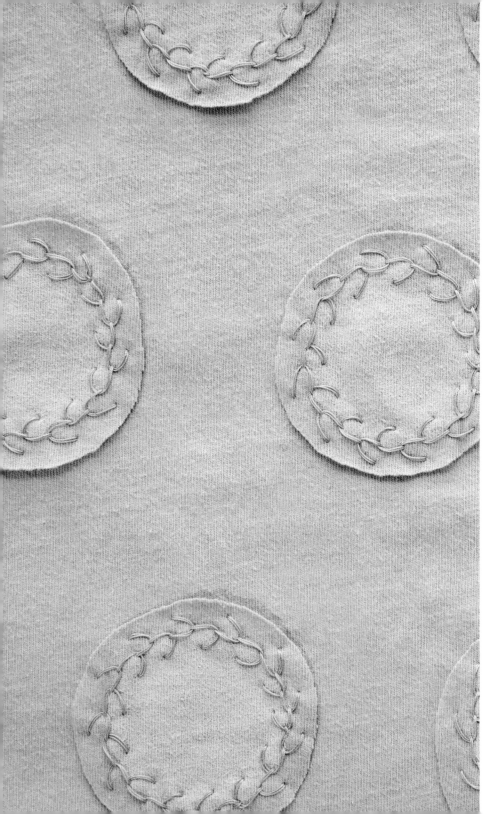

Large Polka Dot Stencil

To create the projects in this book, Large Polka Dot was enlarged 690-percent. This artwork can be photocopied and enlarged from this page, or it can be downloaded full-size from this book's CD or from www.alabamachanin.com.

Index of Beads and Sequins

We use clear, opaque, and satin-finished glass bugle, chop, and seed beads to embellish our garments. Bugle beads are elongated cylindrical beads; chop beads are cut bugle beads; and seed beads are very small, rounded beads. We stitch beads to our garments using the same button craft thread (see page 132) that we use for construction and embroidery, but with a single, rather than a double, strand of thread since a doubled thread tends to tangle excessively when embellishing with beads; however, if you are constructing a seam with a beaded stitch, you will want to use a double strand to add strength to your seams. Either way, we secure the thread with at least two double knots (see page 133) for a double strand and up to six knots for a single strand. We use a #10 milliner's needle because it accommodates our thicker thread while still passing through the beads' small holes. Always test a threaded needle with your beads to make sure they work well together before starting a project. You may want to pick up one or more beads with each of your stitches, depending on how many beads will fit your stitch and the design of your project. Sometimes we also embellish with flat, round 4 to 6 mm sequins, either on their own or in combination with beads. We attach sequins with a single strand of button craft thread, securing the thread with at least two double knots. When we place sequins ¼" (6 mm) or closer together, we sew them with one continuous thread. If they are further apart, we knot off the thread for each sequin separately.

Following is a visual guide to some of our favorite techniques for embellishing with beads and sequins. We also work our decorative stitches with beads (see pages 142-143), often on necklines. And we sometimes embellish the hemlines on skirts, dresses, and sleeves (as shown on the skirt on page 113).

Accent Embellishment
Stitch sequins and/or beads to fabric so they appear to have been dropped in clusters. In this example we distributed sequins throughout the stencil shapes.

Full Beading

Fill an area completely with beads in a random or ordered layout.

Half (or Partial) Beading

Partially fill an area with beads in a random or ordered layout.

Armor Beading and Embellishment

A mixture of sequins and beads. Here we combined sequins, bugle beads, and chop beads for random mixed beading.

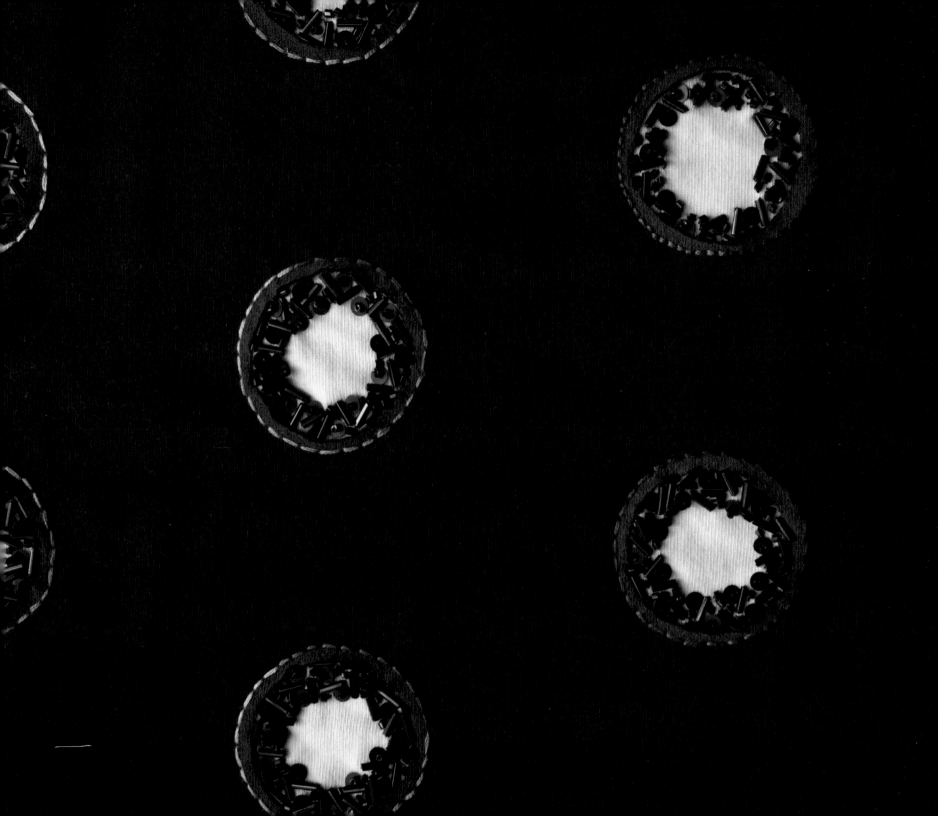

Beading Glove

To keep beads close at hand while you're working, try this ingenious beading glove designed by stitcher Wanita Lawler.

SUPPLIES

3" x 6" (7.5 cm x 15 cm) piece ribbing fabric (cut from old T-shirt so fabric's grain line runs parallel to 3" (7.5 cm) side

Double-stick tape

1. Fold ribbing in half with wrong sides together, so it measures 3" (7.5 cm) square.

2. Stitch the raw edges opposite fold together ¼" (6 mm) from edge. Fold the seam allowances over to one side, and stitch down with a felled seam (see page 145).

3. Lay the stitched tube flat, with the seam at one side. On the folded edge opposite the felled seam, measure 1" (2.5 cm) down from top edge, and cut ½" (12 mm) -wide slit toward the seam through both layers.

4. Slip your hand in glove and thumb through slit. Adhere double-sided tape to top of glove. Add beads on top of tape or dip tape into a container of beads.

Inside Beading
Fill with beads an area of reverse applique that has been cut away. Opposite and on the dress on page 15, we worked the beads around the circumference of each dot.

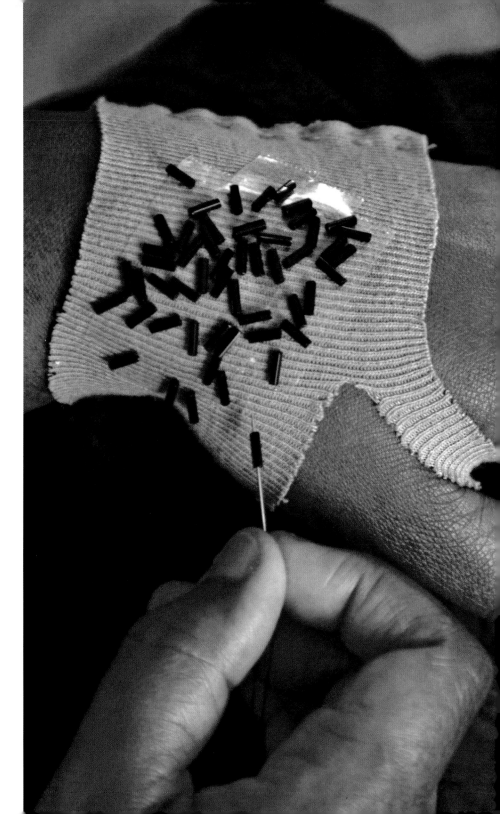

Index of Design Choices

Our design process is, at its essence, a series of choices: garment type, weight and color of fabric, stencil, textile paint color, embroidery techniques, thread and/or floss color, knot position, seam type. Following are details about every choice we made for the fabrics and garments presented in this book. If you have questions, email studio@alabamachanin.com.

P. 2 Garment – Long Evening Dress—Fabric weight – **Medium** | Top-layer fabric – **Black** | Thread – **Black** | Knots – **Inside** | Seams – **Inside Felled** | Binding stitch – **Cretan** | **P. 4** Garment – Alabama Corset | Fabric weight – **Medium** | Top-layer fabric – **Dark Gray** | Bottom-layer fabric – **Dark Gray** | Applique layer – **Natural** | Stencil – **New Leaves** | Treatment – **Whipstitch Applique** | Textile paint – **White Gold** | Thread – **Cream and Gray** | Knots – **Inside** | Seams – **Inside Felled** | Binding stitch – **Cretan** | Garment – Gore Skirt | Fabric weight – **Light** | Top-layer fabric – **Black** | Bottom-layer fabric – **Black** | Stencil – **Magdalena** | Treatment – **Backstitch Reverse Applique** | Textile paint – **Black Gold** | Thread – **Black** | Embroidery floss – **Dark Gray** | Knots – **Inside** | Seams – **Inside Felled** **P. 6 Model 1** Garment – Long Fitted Skirt—Fabric weight – **Light** | Top-layer fabric – **Plum** | Bottom-layer fabric – **Plum** | Stencil – **New Leaves** | Treatment – **Backstitch Negative Reverse Applique** | Textile paint – **Pearl Brownie** | Thread – **Burgundy** | Embroidery floss – **Burgundy** | Knots – **Inside** | Seams – **Inside Felled** | Binding stitch – **Zigzag Chain** | **Model 2** Garment – Long Sleeve Bolero—Fabric weight – **Light** | Top-layer fabric – **Natural** | Thread – **Cream** | Knots – **Inside** | Seams – **Inside Felled** | Binding stitch – **Cretan** | Garment – A-Line Dress | Fabric weight – **Medium** | Top-layer fabric – **Dark Gray** | Thread – **Gray** | Knots – **Inside** | Seams – **Outside Felled** | Binding stitch – **Zigzag Chain**

P. 9 Garment – Gore Skirt—Fabric weight – **Medium** | Top-layer fabric – **Natural Plum** | Bottom-layer fabric – **Natural Plum** | Stencil – **Large Polka Dots** | Treatment – **Featherstitch Negative Reverse Applique** | Textile paint – **Natural Plum** | Thread – **Tan** | Knots – **Inside** | Seams – **Inside Felled** | Binding stitch – **Zigzag Chain** | Garment – Poncho—Fabric weight – **Medium** | Top-layer fabric – **Natural** | Thread – **Cream** | Knots – **Outside** | Seams – **Outside Floating** | **Model 1** | Garment – Poncho—Fabric weight – **Medium** | Top-layer fabric – **Black** | Bottom-layer fabric – **Black** | Stencil – **Magdalena** | Treatment – **Negative Reverse Applique** | Textile paint – **White Gold** | Thread – **Black** | Knots – **Outside** | Seams – **Outside Floating** | **Model 2** | Garment – Long Evening Dress—Fabric weight – **Light** | Top-layer fabric – **Black** | Bottom Layer – **Black** | Stencil – **New Leaves** | Treatment – **Backstitch Reverse Applique** | Textile paint – **Black Gold** | Thread – **Black** | Embroidery floss – **Dark Gray** | Knots – **Inside** | Seams – **Inside Felled** | Binding stitch – **Cretan**

Part 1 | Alabama Chanin Garments

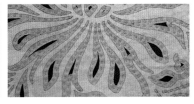

P. 12 Garment – A-Line Dress—Fabric weight – **Medium** | Top-layer fabric – **Black** | Bottom-layer fabric – **Black** | Stencil – **New Leaves** | Treatment – **Backstitch Reverse Applique** | Textile paint – **Black Gold** | Thread – **Black** | Embroidery floss – **Dark Gray** | Knots – **Inside** | Seams – **Inside Felled** | Garment – A-Line Top—Fabric weight – **Light** | Top-layer fabric – **Pewter** | Thread – **Gray** | Knots – **Inside** | Seams – **Inside Felled** | Binding stitch – **Cretan** | Garment – Long Fitted Skirt—Fabric weight – **Light** | Top-layer fabric – **Plum** | Bottom-layer fabric – **Plum** | Stencil – **New Leaves** | Treatment – **Backstitch Negative Reverse Applique** | Textile paint – **Pearl Brownie** | Thread – **Burgundy** | Embroidery floss – **Burgundy** | Knots – **Inside** | Seams – **Inside Felled** | Binding stitch – **Zigzag Chain** | Garment – Swatch—Fabric weight – **Medium** | Top-layer fabric – **Natural Blue Gray** | Bottom-layer fabric – **Black** | Stencil – **Magdalena** | Treatment – **Inked Reverse Applique** | Textile paint – **Nickel** | Thread – **Gray** | Knots – **Inside**

P. 14 Model 1 | Garment – Classic Wrap Skirt—Fabric weight – **Medium** | Top-layer fabric – **Natural Blue Gray** | Bottom-layer fabric – **Natural Blue Gray** | Thread – **Gray** | Knots – **Inside** | Seams – **Inside Felled** | **Model 2** | Garment – Tank Tunic —Fabric weight – **Medium** | Top-layer fabric – **Dark Gray** | Bottom-layer fabric – **Dark Gray** | Thread – **Gray** | Knots – **Inside** | Seams – **Inside Felled** | Binding stitch – **Cretan** | Garment – Mid-Length Skirt—Fabric weight – **Medium** | Top-layer fabric – **Steel** | Bottom-layer fabric – **Steel** | Thread – **Gray** | Knots – **Inside** | Seams – **Inside Felled** | Binding stitch – **Zigzag Chain P. 15 Model 1** | Garment – A-Line Dress—Fabric weight – **Medium** | Top-layer fabric – **Black** | Bottom-layer fabric – **Black** | Stencil – **Large Polka Dots** | Treatment – **Reverse Applique with Inside Armor Beading** | Textile paint – **White Gold** | Thread – **Black** | Embroidery floss – **Black Varigated** | Knots – **Inside** | Seams – **Inside Felled** | Bugle beads – **Black** | Chop beads – **Black** | Sequins – **Black** | Binding stitch – **Cretan** | **Model 2** | Garment – Long A-Line Dress—Fabric weight – **Medium** | Top-layer fabric – **Dark Indigo** | Thread – **Gray** | Knots – **Inside** | Seams – **Inside Felled** | Binding stitch – **Rosebud** | **Model 3** | Garment – A-Line Vest with Pockets—Fabric weight – **Medium** | Top-layer fabric – **Black** | Thread – **Black** | Knots – **Inside** | Seams – **Inside Felled** | Binding stitch – **Cretan** | Garment – A-Line Tunic—Fabric weight – **Medium** | Top-layer fabric – **Natural** | Thread – **Cream** | Knots – **Inside** | Seams – **Inside Felled** | Binding stitch – **Whipstitch** | **Model 4** | Garment – A-Line Dress—Fabric weight – **Medium** | Top-layer fabric – **Black** | Bottom-layer fabric – **Black** | Stencil – **New Leaves** | Treatment – **Backstitch Reverse Applique** | Textile paint – **Black Gold** | Thread – **Black** | Embroidery floss – **Dark Gray** | Knots – **Inside** | Seams – **Inside Felled** | Binding stitch – **Cretan**

P. 16 Garment – A-Line Tunic—Fabric weight – **Medium** | Top-layer fabric – **Natural** | Thread – **Cream** | Knots – **Inside** | Seams – **Inside Felled** | Binding stitch – **Whipstitch** | Garment – Classic Wrap Skirt—Fabric weight – **Medium** | Top-layer fabric – **Natural Blue Gray** | Bottom-layer fabric – **Natural Blue Gray** | Thread – **Gray** | Knots – **Inside** | Seams – **Inside Felled** **P. 18** Garment – A-Line Dress—Fabric weight – **Medium** | Top-layer fabric – **Black** | Bottom-layer fabric – **Black** | Stencil – **New Leaves** | Treatment – **Backstitch**

Reverse Applique | Textile paint – **Black Gold** | Thread – **Black** | Embroidery floss – **Dark Gray** | Knots – **Inside** | Seams – **Inside Felled** | Binding stitch – **Cretan P. 21** Garment – Long A-Line Dress—Fabric weight – **Medium** | Top-layer fabric – **Dark Indigo** | Thread – **Gray** | Knots – **Inside** | Seams – **Inside Felled** | Binding stitch – **Rosebud P. 23** Garment – A-Line Dress—Fabric weight – **Medium** | Top-layer fabric – **Ballet** | Thread – **Tan** | Knots – **Inside** | Seams – **Inside Felled** | Binding stitch – **Cretan**

P. 24-25 Garment – Long Evening Dress—Fabric weight – **Light** | Top-layer fabric – **Black** | Bottom-layer fabric – **Black** | Stencil – **New Leaves** | Treatment – **Backstitch Reverse Applique** | Textile paint – **Black Gold** | Thread – **Black** | Embroidery floss – **Dark Gray** | Knots – **Inside** | Seams – **Inside Felled** | Binding stitch – **Cretan**

P. 26 Garment – A-Line Vest with Patch Pockets—Fabric weight – **Medium** | Top-layer fabric – **Black** | Thread – **Black** | Knots – **Inside** | Seams – **Inside Felled** | Binding stitch – **Cretan** | Garment – A-Line Tunic—Fabric weight – **Medium** | Top-layer fabric – **Natural** | Thread – **Cream** | Knots – **Inside** | Seams – **Inside Felled** | Binding stitch – **Whipstitch** | Garment – Classic Wrap Skirt—Fabric weight – **Medium** | Top-layer fabric – **Natural Blue Gray** | Bottom-layer fabric – **Natural Blue Gray** | Thread – **Gray** | Knots – **Inside** | Seams – **Inside Felled** **P. 27** Garment – Piped A-Line Tunic—Fabric weight – **Medium** | Top-layer fabric – **Natural Plum and Really Red with Dark Gray Piping** | Thread – **Tan** | Knots – **Inside** | Seams – **Inside Floating** | Binding stitch – **Cretan** | Garment – Long Fitted Skirt with Train—Fabric weight – **Medium** | Top-layer fabric – **Steel** | Bottom-layer fabric – **Steel** | Thread – **Gray** | Knots – **Inside** | Seams – **Inside Felled** | Binding stitch – **Zigzag Chain P. 29** Garment – A-Line Dress with Pockets—Fabric weight – **Medium** | Top-layer fabric – **Black** | Pocket fabric – **Really Red** | Thread – **Black and Red** | Knots – **Inside** | Seams – **Inside Felled** | Binding stitch – **Cretan**

P. 30 Model 1 | Garment – Classic Cardigan—Fabric weight – **Medium** | Top-layer fabric – **Dark Gray** | Bottom-layer fabric – **Dark Gray** | Thread – **Gray** | Knots – **Inside** | Seams – **Inside Felled** | Binding stitch – **Cretan** | Garment – A-Line Tunic—Fabric weight – **Medium** | Top-layer fabric – **Natural** | Thread – **Cream** | Knots – **Inside** | Seams – **Inside Felled** | Binding stitch – **Whipstitch** | Garment – Classic Wrap Skirt—Fabric weight – **Medium** | Top-layer fabric – **Dark Gray** | Bottom-layer fabric – **Dark Gray** | Thread – **Gray** | Knots – **Inside** | Seams – **Inside Felled** | **Model 2** | Garment – Classic Jacket—Fabric weight – **Medium** | Top-layer fabric – **Dark Gray** | Bottom-layer fabric – **Dark Gray** | Thread – **Gray** | Knots – **Inside** | Seams – **Inside Felled** | Binding stitch – **Cretan** | Garment – A-Line Top—Fabric weight – **Light** | Top-layer fabric – **Black** | Thread – **Black** | Knots – **Inside** | Seams – **Inside Felled** | Binding stitch – **Cretan** | Garment – Classic Wrap Skirt—Fabric weight – **Medium** | Top-layer fabric – **Dark Indigo** | Bottom-layer fabric – **Dark Indigo** | Stencil – **New Leaves** | Treatment – **Backstitch Reverse Applique** | Textile paint – **Pearl Charcoal** | Thread – **Gray** | Embroidery floss – **Dark Gray** | Knots – **Inside** | Seams – **Inside Felled** | **Model 3** | Garment – Classic Coat—Fabric weight – **Medium** | Top-layer fabric – **Dark Gray** | Bottom-layer fabric – **Dark Gray** | Thread – **Gray** | Knots – **Inside** | Seams – **Inside Felled** | Binding stitch – **Featherstitch** | Garment – Shell Top—Fabric weight – **Light** | Top-layer fabric – **Natural** | Thread – **Cream** | Knots – **Inside** | Seams – **Inside Felled** | Binding stitch – **Cretan** | Garment – Classic Wrap Skirt—Fabric weight – **Medium** | Top-layer fabric – **Natural Blue Gray** | Bottom-layer fabric – **Natural Blue Gray** | Thread – **Gray** | Knots – **Inside** | Seams – **Inside Felled P. 32** Garment – Classic Coat—Fabric weight – **Medium** | Top-layer fabric – **Dark Gray** | Bottom-layer fabric – **Dark Gray** | Thread – **Gray** | Knots – **Inside** | Seams – **Inside Felled** | Binding stitch – **Featherstitch P. 34** Garment – Peplum Cardigan—Fabric weight – **Medium** | Top-layer fabric – **Dark Gray** | Bottom-layer fabric – **Dark Gray** | Stencil – **New Leaves** | Treatment – **Backstitch Reverse Applique** | Textile paint – **Black Gold** | Thread – **Gray** | Embroidery floss – **Dark Gray** | Knots – **Inside** | Seams – **Inside Felled** | Binding stitch – **Zigzag Chain** | **P. 35** Garment – A-Line Dress—Fabric weight – **Medium** | Top-layer fabric – **Black** | Bottom-layer fabric – **Black** | Stencil – **New Leaves** | Treatment – **Backstitch Reverse Applique** | Textile paint – **Black Gold** | Thread – **Black** | Embroidery floss – **Dark Gray** | Knots – **Inside** | Seams – **Inside Felled** | Binding stitch – **Cretan**

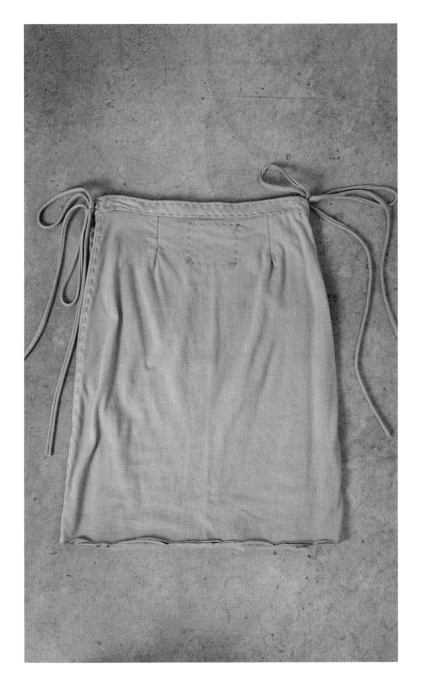

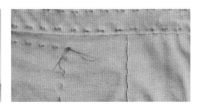

P. 36 Garment – Classic Wrap Skirt—Fabric weight – **Medium** | Top-layer fabric – **Natural Blue Gray** | Bottom-layer fabric – **Natural Blue Gray** | Thread – **Gray** | Knots – **Inside** | Seams – **Inside Felled** P. 38 Garment – A-Line Top—Fabric weight – **Medium** | Top-layer fabric – **Navy** | Thread – **Navy** | Knots – **Inside** | Seams – **Outside Floating** | Binding stitch – **Cretan** | Garment – Classic Wrap Skirt—Fabric weight – **Medium** | Top-layer fabric – **Dark Indigo** | Bottom-layer fabric – **Dark Indigo** | Stencil – **New Leaves** | Treatment – **Backstitch Reverse Applique** | Textile paint – **Pearl Charcoal** | Thread – **Gray** | Embroidery floss – **Dark Gray** | Knots – **Inside** | Seams – **Inside Felled** P. 41 Garment – Shell Top—Fabric weight – **Light** | Top-layer fabric – **Natural** | Thread – **Cream** | Knots – **Inside** | Seams – **Inside Felled** | Binding stitch – **Cretan** | Garment – Classic Wrap Skirt—Fabric weight – **Medium** | Top-layer fabric – **Natural Blue Gray** | Bottom-layer fabric – **Natural Blue Gray** | Thread – **Gray** | Knots – **Inside** | Seams – **Inside Felled**

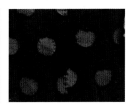

P. 42 Garment – Long Sleeve Bolero—Fabric weight – **Medium** | Top-layer fabric – **Steel** | Bottom-layer fabric – **Steel** | Thread – **Gray** | Knots – **Inside** | Seams – **Inside Felled** | Binding stitch – **Cretan** | Garment – Fitted Top—Fabric weight – **Medium** | Top-layer fabric – **Dark Gray** | Bottom-layer fabric – **Dark Gray** | Thread – **Gray** | Knots – **Inside** | Seams – **Inside Felled** | Binding stitch – **Cretan** | Garment – Long Fitted Skirt with Train—Fabric weight – **Medium** | Top-layer fabric – **Black** | Bottom-layer fabric – **Black** | Stencil – **Large Polka Dots** | Treatment – **Negative Reverse Applique** | Textile paint – **White Gold** | Thread – **Black** | Knots – **Inside** | Seams – **Inside Felled** | Binding stitch – **Zigzag Chain** P. 45 Model 1 | Garment – T-Shirt Top—Fabric weight – **Medium** | Top-layer fabric – **Steel** | Thread – **Gray** | Knots – **Inside** | Seams – **Inside Felled** | Binding stitch – **Cretan** | Garment – Classic Wrap Skirt—Fabric weight – **Medium** | Top-layer fabric – **Dark Gray** | Bottom-layer fabric – **Dark Gray** | Thread – **Gray** | Knots – **Inside** | Seams – **Inside Felled** | Model 2 | Garment – Shell Top—Fabric weight – **Light** | Top-layer fabric – **Natural** | Thread – **Cream** | Knots – **Inside** | Seams – **Inside Felled** | Binding stitch – **Cretan** | Garment – Classic Wrap Skirt—Fabric weight – **Medium** | Top-layer fabric – **Natural Blue Gray** | Bottom-layer fabric – **Natural Blue Gray** | Thread – **Gray** | Knots – **Inside** | Seams – **Inside**

Felled | **P. 47** Garment – Shell Top—Fabric weight – **Light** | Top-layer fabric – **Ballet** | Bottom-layer fabric – **Natural** | Stencil – **Magdalena** | Treatment – **Backstitch Reverse Applique** | Textile paint – **Ecru** | Thread – **Tan** | Embroidery floss – **Tea** | Knots – **Inside** | Seams – **Inside Felled** | Binding stitch – **Cretan** | Garment – Pleated Skirt—Fabric weight – **Medium** | Top-layer fabric – **Natural Blue Gray** | Bottom-layer fabric – **Natural Blue Gray** | Stencil – **Whispering Rose** | Treatment – **Reverse Applique** | Textile paint – **Nickel** | Thread – **Gray** | Knots – **Outside** | Seams – **Inside Felled and Outside Floating** | Binding stitch – **Zigzag Chain P. 48** Garment – Shell Top with Godets—Fabric weight – **Medium** | Top-layer fabric – **Black** | Bottom-layer fabric – **Black** | Thread – **Black** | Knots – **Inside** | Seams – **Outside Floating** | Binding stitch – **Whipstitch**

P. 50-51 Garment – Fitted Long Sleeve T-Shirt with Princess Seams—Fabric weight – **Light** | Top-layer fabric – **Dark Indigo** | Bottom-layer fabric – **Dark Indigo** | Stencil – **Magdalena** | Treatment – **Backstitch Reverse Applique** | Textile paint – **Pearl Charcoal** | Thread – **Gray** | Embroidery floss – **Dark Gray** | Knots – **Inside** | Seams – **Inside Felled** | Binding stitch – **Cretan** | Garment – Mid-Length Skirt—Fabric weight – **Medium** | Top-layer fabric – **Black** | Thread – **Black** | Knots – **Inside** | Seams – **Inside Felled** | Binding stitch – **Zigzag Chain P. 52** Garment – Shell Top with Stripe—Fabric weight – **Medium** | Top-layer fabric – **Dark Indigo and Natural Blue Gray** | Thread – **Gray** | Knots – **Inside** | Seams – **Outside Floating** | Binding stitch – **Cretan** | Garment – Swing Skirt—Fabric weight – **Medium** | Top-layer fabric – **Natural** | Bottom-layer fabric – **Natural** | Thread – **Cream** | Knots – **Inside** | Seams – **Inside Felled** | Binding stitch – **Zigzag Chain P. 53** Garment – Shell Top with Stripe—Fabric weight – **Medium** | Top-layer fabric – **Dark Indigo and Natural Blue Gray** | Thread – **Gray** | Knots – **Inside** | Seams – **Outside Floating** | Binding stitch – **Cretan**

P. 54 Garment – Long Sleeve Bolero—Fabric weight – **Light** | Top-layer fabric – **Natural** | Thread – **Cream** | Knots – **Inside** | Seams – **Inside Felled** | Binding stitch – **Cretan** | Garment – A-Line Dress—Fabric weight – **Medium** | Top-layer fabric – **Dark Gray** | Thread – **Gray** | Knots – **Inside** | Seams – **Outside Felled** |

Binding stitch – **Zigzag Chain P. 57 Model 1** | Garment – Long Sleeve Bolero—Fabric weight – **Light** | Top-layer fabric – **Natural** | Thread – **Cream** | Knots – **Inside** | Seams – **Inside Felled** | Binding stitch – **Cretan** | Garment – A-Line Dress—Fabric weight – **Medium** | Top-layer fabric – **Dark Gray** | Thread – **Gray** | Knots – **Inside** | Seams – **Outside Felled** | Binding stitch – **Zigzag Chain** | **Model 2** | Garment – Long Sleeve Bolero—Fabric weight – **Medium** | Top-layer fabric – **Steel** | Bottom-layer fabric – **Steel** | Thread – **Gray** | Knots – **Inside** | Seams – **Inside Felled** | Binding stitch – **Cretan** | Garment – Camisole Babydoll Dress—Fabric weight – **Medium** | Top-layer fabric – **Dark Gray** | Bottom-layer fabric – **Dark Gray** | Thread – **Gray** | Knots – **Inside** | Seams – **Inside Felled** | Binding stitch – **Zigzag Chain and Cretan P. 58** Garment – Fitted Dress—Fabric weight – **Medium** | Top-layer fabric – **Steel** | Bottom-layer fabric – **Steel** | Thread – **Gray** | Knots – **Inside** | Seams – **Inside Felled** | Binding stitch – **Cretan** | Garment – Swing Skirt—Fabric weight – **Medium** | Top-layer fabric – **Natural** | Bottom-layer fabric – **Natural** | Thread – **Cream** | Knots – **Inside** | Seams – **Inside Felled** | Binding stitch – **Zigzag Chain**

P. 60 Garment – Long Fitted Skirt with Train—Fabric weight – **Medium** | Top-layer fabric – **Navy** | Bottom-layer fabric – **Black** | Stencil – **Magdalena** | Treatment – **Negative Reverse Applique** | Textile paint – **Navy** | Thread – **Navy** | Knots – **Outside** | Seams – **Inside Felled** | Binding stitch – **Zigzag Chain P. 63** Garment – Fitted Skirt with Patch Pockets—Fabric weight – **Medium** | Top-layer fabric – **Black** | Bottom-layer fabric – **Black** | Stencil – **Magdalena** | Treatment – **Reverse Applique** | Textile paint – **Black** | Thread – **Black** | Knots – **Inside** | Seams – **Inside Felled** | Binding stitch – **Zigzag Chain**

P. 64 Garment – Long A-Line Dress—Fabric weight – **Medium** | Top-layer fabric – **Black** | Thread – **Black** | Knots – **Inside** | Seams – **Inside Felled** | Binding stitch – **Cretan** | Garment – Poncho—Fabric weight – **Medium** | Top-layer fabric – **Black** | Bottom-layer fabric – **Black** | Stencil – **Magdalena** | Treatment – **Negative Reverse Applique** | Textile paint – **White Gold** | Thread – **Black** | Knots – **Outside** | Seams – **Outside Floating P. 66** Garment – Tank Tunic—Fabric weight – **Medium** | Top-layer fabric – **Dark Gray** | Bottom-layer fabric – **Dark**

Gray | Thread – **Gray** | Knots – **Inside** | Seams – **Inside Felled** | Binding stitch – **Cretan** | Garment – Gore Skirt—Fabric weight – **Light** | Top-layer fabric – **Black** | Bottom-layer fabric – **Black** | Stencil – **Magdalena** | Treatment – **Backstitch Reverse Applique** | Textile paint – **Black Gold** | Thread – **Black** | Embroidery floss – **Dark Gray** | Knots – **Inside** | Seams – **Inside Felled** | Binding stitch – **Zigzag Chain P. 69** Garment – Camisole Dress—Fabric weight – **Medium** | Top-layer fabric – **Plum** | Bottom-layer fabric – **Plum** | Thread – **Burgundy** | Knots – **Inside** | Seams – **Inside Felled** | Stitch – **Cretan P. 71** Garment – Camisole Top—Fabric weight – **Medium** | Top-layer fabric – **Steel** | Bottom-layer fabric – **Steel** | Thread – **Gray** | Knots – **Inside** | Seams – **Inside Felled** | Binding stitch – **Cretan** | Garment – Mid-Length Skirt—Fabric weight – **Medium** | Top-layer fabric – **Dark**

Gray | Bottom-layer fabric – **Dark Gray** | Thread – **Gray** | Knots – **Inside** | Seams – **Inside Felled** | Binding stitch – **Zigzag Chain P. 72** Garment – Alabama Corset—Fabric weight – **Medium** | Top-layer fabric – **Natural** | Bottom-layer fabric – **Natural** | Treatment – **Chain Stitch Embroidery** | Thread – **Cream** | Embroidery floss – **Black** | Knots – **Inside** | Seams – **Inside Felled** | Binding stitch – **Cretan** | Garment – Panel Tank—Fabric weight – **Medium** | Top-layer fabric – **Natural** | Thread – **Cream** | Knots – **Inside** | Seams – **Inside Felled** | Binding stitch – **Cretan** | Garment – Fitted Skirt with Patch Pockets—Fabric weight – **Medium** | Top-layer fabric – **Black** | Bottom-layer fabric – **Black** | Stencil – **Magdalena** | Treatment – **Reverse Applique** | Textile paint – **Black** | Thread – **Black** | Knots – **Inside** | Seams – **Inside Felled** | Binding stitch – **Zigzag Chain**

P. 74 Garment – Alabama Corset—Fabric weight – **Medium** | Top-layer fabric – **Black** | Bottom-layer fabric – **Peacock** | Stencil – **Small Polka Dots** | Treatment – **Backstitch Reverse Applique** | Textile paint – **White Gold** | Thread – **Black** | Embroidery floss – **Black Varigated** | Knots – **Inside** | Seams – **Inside Felled** | Binding stitch – **Cretan P. 75** Garment –Alabama Corset—Fabric weight – **Medium** | Top-layer fabric – **Natural Plum** | Thread – **Tan** | Knots – **Inside** | Seams – **Outside Floating** | Binding stitch – **Herringbone** | **Model 1 |** Garment – Alabama Corset—Fabric weight – **Medium** | Top-layer fabric – **Black** | Bottom-layer fabric – **Black** | Stencil – **Magdalena** | Treatment – **Reverse Applique** | Textile paint – **Black** | Thread – **Black** | Knots – **Inside** | Seams – **Inside Felled** | Binding stitch – **Cretan** | Garment – Panel Tank—Fabric weight – **Medium** | Top-layer fabric – **Navy** | Thread – **Navy** | Knots – **Inside** | Seams – **Inside Felled** | Binding stitch – **Cretan** | Garment – Classic Wrap Skirt—Fabric weight – **Medium** | Top-layer fabric – **Natural Blue Gray** | Bottom-layer fabric – **Natural Blue Gray** | Thread – **Gray** | Knots – **Inside** | Seams – **Inside Felled P. 76** Garment – Swing Skirt—Fabric weight – **Medium** | Top-layer fabric – **Natural Blue Gray** | Bottom-layer fabric – **Natural** | Stencil – **Magdalena** | Treatment – **Reverse Applique** | Textile paint – **Nickel** | Thread – **Gray** | Knots – **Inside** | Seams – **Inside Felled** | Binding stitch – **Zigzag Chain P. 77** Garment – Scoop Neck Top—Fabric weight – **Medium** | Top-layer fabric – **Black** | Bottom-layer fabric – **Black** | Stencil – **Magdalena** | Treatment – **Reverse Applique** | Textile paint – **Black** | Thread – **Black** | Knots – **Outside** | Seams – **Inside Felled** | Binding stitch – **Cretan** | Garment – Panel Tank—Fabric weight – **Medium** | Top-layer fabric – **Ballet** | Thread – **Tan** | Knots – **Inside** | Seams – **Inside Felled** | Binding stitch – **Cretan** | Garment – Swing Skirt—Fabric weight – **Medium** | Top-layer fabric – **Ballet** | Bottom-layer fabric – **Ballet** | Stencil – **Magdalena** | Treatment – **Backstitch Reverse Applique** | Textile paint – **Ecru** | Thread – **Tan** | Embroidery floss – **Tea** | Knots – **Inside** | Seams – **Inside Felled** | Binding stitch – **Zigzag Chain**

Part 2 | Fit + Customization

P. 78 Model 1 | Garment – Classic Cardigan—Fabric weight – **Medium** | Top-layer fabric – **Dark Gray** | Bottom-layer fabric – **Dark Gray** | Thread – **Gray** | Knots – **Inside** | Seams – **Inside Felled** | Binding stitch – **Cretan** | Garment – Alabama Corset—Fabric weight – **Medium** | Top-layer fabric – **Really Red with Coral and Apple Piping** | Thread – **Tan** | Knots – **Inside** | Seams – **Outside Floating** | Binding stitch – **Double Cretan** | **Model 2** | Garment – Long Sleeve Bolero—Fabric weight – **Medium** | Top-layer fabric – **Steel** | Bottom-layer fabric – **Steel** | Thread – **Gray** | Knots – **Inside** | Seams – **Inside Felled** | Binding stitch – **Cretan** | Garment – Fitted Dress—Fabric weight – **Medium** | Top-layer fabric – **Dove** | Bottom-layer fabric – **Dove** | Thread – **Gray** | Knots – **Inside** | Seams – **Inside Felled** | Binding stitch – **Cretan** | **Model 3** | Garment – Classic Cardigan—Fabric weight – **Medium** | Top-layer fabric – **Natural Blue Gray** | Bottom-layer fabric – **Natural Blue Gray** | Thread – **Gray** | Knots – **Inside** | Seams – **Inside Felled** | Binding stitch – **Cretan** | Garment – Alabama Corset—Fabric weight – **Medium** | Top-layer fabric – **Natural Plum** | Thread – **Tan** | Knots – **Inside** | Seams – **Outside Floating** | Binding stitch – **Herringbone P. 80 Model 1** | Garment – Tank Tunic—Fabric weight – **Medium** | Top-layer fabric – **Dark Gray** | Bottom-layer fabric – **Dark Gray** | Thread – **Gray** | Knots – **Inside** | Seams – **Inside Felled** | Binding stitch – **Cretan** | Garment – Mid-Length Skirt—Fabric weight – **Medium** | Top-layer fabric – **Steel** | Bottom-layer fabric – **Steel** | Thread – **Gray** | Knots – **Inside** | Seams – **Inside Felled** | Binding stitch – **Zigzag Chain** | **Model 2** | Garment – Long A-Line Dress—Fabric weight – **Medium** | Top-layer fabric – **Black** | Bottom-layer fabric – **Black** | Thread – **Black** | Knots – **Inside** | Seams – **Inside Felled** | Binding stitch – **Cretan P. 85** Garment – V-neck Shell Top—Fabric weight – **Light** | Top-layer fabric – **Black** | Bottom-layer fabric – **Black** | Stencil – **Magdalena** | Treatment – **Backstitch Reverse Applique** | Textile paint – **Black** | Thread – **Black** | Embroidery floss – **Black** | Knots – **Inside** | Seams – **Inside Felled** | Binding stitch – **Cretan** | Garment – Pleated Skirt—Fabric weight – **Medium** | Top-layer fabric – **Navy** | Bottom-layer fabric – **Navy** | Stencil – **Whispering Rose** | Treatment – **Reverse Applique** | Textile paint – **Navy** | Thread – **Navy** | Knots – **Outside** | Seams – **Inside Felled and Outside Floating** | Binding stitch – **Zigzag Chain P. 89** Garment – Fitted Top— Fabric weight – **Medium** | Top-layer fabric – **Dark Gray** | Bottom-layer fabric – **Dark Gray** | Thread – **Gray** | Knots – **Inside** | Seams – **Inside Felled** | Binding stitch – **Cretan**

P. 95 Garment – Classic Wrap Skirt with Border— Fabric weight – **Medium** | Top-layer fabric – **Natural Blue Gray** | Bottom-layer fabric – **Natural Blue Gray** | Border Fabric – **Dusk** | Thread – **Gray** | Knots – **Inside** | Seams – **Inside Felled P. 96** Garment – A-Line Dress—Fabric weight – **Medium** | Top-layer fabric – **White** | Thread – **White** | Knots – **Inside** | Seams – **Inside Felled** | Binding stitch – **Cretan**

P. 101 Garment – Shell Top with Darts—Fabric weight – **Medium** | Top-layer fabric – **Natural** | Thread – **Cream** | Knots – **Inside** | Seams – **Inside Felled** | Binding stitch – **Cretan** | Garment – Gore Skirt—Fabric weight – **Light** | Top-layer fabric – **Black** | Bottom-layer fabric – **Black** | Stencil – **Magdalena** | Treatment – **Backstitch Reverse Applique** | Textile paint – **Black Gold** | Thread – **Black** | Embroidery floss – **Dark Gray** | Knots – **Inside** | Seams – **Inside Felled** | Binding stitch – **Zigzag Chain P. 113** Garment – Mid-Length Skirt—Fabric weight – **Light** | Top-layer fabric – **Black** | Treatment – **Beaded** | Thread – **Black** | Knots – **Inside** | Seams – **Inside Felled** | Bugle beads – **Black** | Chop beads – **Black** | Sequins – **Black** | Binding stitch – **Zigzag Chain P. 115** Garment – Classic Coat—Fabric weight – **Medium** | Top-layer fabric – **Pewter** | Bottom-layer fabric – **Black** | Band fabric – **Really Red** | Stencil – **New Leaves** | Treatment – **Backstitch Reverse Applique** | Textile paint – **Black Gold** | Thread – **Gray** | Embroidery floss – **Dark Gray** | Knots – **Inside** | Seams – **Inside Felled** | Binding stitch – **Cretan** | Garment – Tank Tunic—Fabric weight – **Medium** | Top-layer fabric – **Dark Gray** | Bottom-layer fabric – **Dark Gray** | Thread – **Gray** | Knots – **Inside** | Seams – **Inside Felled** | Binding stitch – **Cretan** | Garment – Gore Skirt—Fabric weight – **Light** | Top-layer fabric – **Black** | Bottom-layer fabric – **Black** | Stencil – **Magdalena** | Treatment – **Backstitch** | **Reverse Applique** | Textile paint – **Black Gold** | Thread – **Black** | Embroidery floss – **Dark Gray** | Knots – **Inside** | Seams – **Inside Felled** | Binding stitch – **Zigzag Chain**

P. 120 Garment – Camisole Top—Fabric weight – **Medium** | Top-layer fabric – **Steel** | Bottom-layer fabric – **Steel** | Thread – **Gray** | Knots – **Inside** | Seams – **Inside Felled** | Binding stitch – **Cretan P. 123** Garment – Long Sleeve Bolero— Fabric weight – **Medium** | Top-layer fabric – **Steel** | Bottom-layer fabric – **Steel** | Thread – **Gray** | Knots – **Inside** | Seams – **Inside Felled** | Binding stitch – **Cretan** | Garment – Fitted Top—Fabric weight – **Medium** | Top-layer fabric – **Dark Gray** | Bottom-layer fabric – **Dark Gray** | Thread – **Gray** | Knots – **Inside** | Seams – **Inside Felled** | Binding stitch – **Cretan**

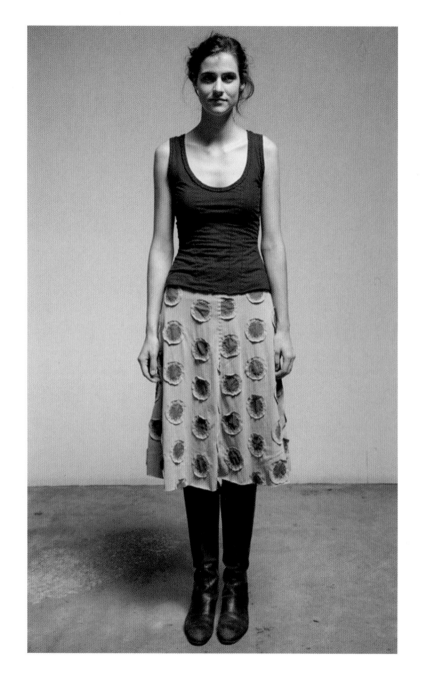

Part 3 | Basic Techniques + Embellishment Glossary

P. 126 Garment – Swing Skirt—Fabric weight – **Medium** | Top-layer fabric – **Natural Blue Gray** | Bottom-layer fabric – **Natural** | Stencil – **Magdalena** | Treatment – **Reverse Applique** | Textile paint – **Nickel** | Thread – **Gray** | Knots – **Inside** | Garment – Long-Fitted Skirt—Fabric weight – **Medium** | Top-layer fabric – **Navy** | Bottom-layer fabric – **Black** | Stencil – **Magdalena** | Treatment – **Negative Reverse Applique** | Textile paint – **Navy** | Thread – **Navy** | Knots – **Outside P. 133** Garment – Swatch—Fabric weight – **Medium** | Top-layer fabric – **Navy** | Bottom-layer fabric – **Black** | Stencil – **Magdalena** | Treatment – **Negative Reverse Applique** | Textile paint – **Navy** | Thread – **Navy** | Knots – **Outside**

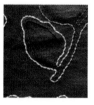

P. 137 Garment – Classic Coat—Fabric weight – **Medium** | Top-layer fabric – **Dark Gray** | Bottom-layer fabric – **Dark Gray** | Thread – **Gray** | Knots – **Inside** | Seams – **Inside Felled** | Binding stitch – **Featherstitch** | Garment – Shell Top—Fabric weight – **Light** |Top-layer fabric – **Natural** | Thread – **Cream** | Knots – **Inside** | Seams – **Inside Felled** | Binding stitch – **Cretan** | Garment – Classic Wrap Skirt—Fabric weight – **Medium** | Top-layer fabric – **Natural Blue Gray** | Bottom-layer fabric – **Natural Blue Gray** | Thread – **Gray** | Knots – **Inside** | Seams – **Inside Felled** **P. 142** Garment – Classic Coat—Fabric weight – **Medium** | Top-layer fabric – **Pewter** | Bottom-layer fabric – **Black** | Band Fabric – **Really Red** | Stencil – **New Leaves** | Treatment – **Backstitch Reverse Applique** | Textile paint – **Black Gold** | Thread – **Gray** | Embroidery floss – **Dark Gray** | Knots – **Inside** | Seams – **Inside Felled** | Binding stitch – **Cretan P. 150** Garment – Long Evening Dress—Fabric weight – **Light** | Top-layer fabric – **Black** | Bottom-layer fabric – **Black** | Stencil – **New Leaves** | Treatment – **Backstitch Reverse Applique** | Textile paint – **Black Gold** | Embroidery floss – **Variegated Black Floss** | Knots – **Inside** | Garment – Long Fitted Skirt—Fabric weight – **Light** | Top-layer fabric – **Plum** | Bottom-layer fabric – **Plum** | Stencil – **New Leaves** | Treatment – **Backstitch Negative Reverse Applique** | Textile paint – **Pearl Brownie** | Thread – **Burgundy** | Embroidery floss – **Burgundy** | Knots – **Inside** | Seams – **Inside Felled** | Binding stitch – **Zigzag Chain**

P. 153 Garment – Swatch—Fabric weight – **Medium** | Top-layer fabric – **Black** | Bottom-layer fabric – **Black** | Applique layer – **Natural** | Stencil – **Magdalena** | Treatment – **Whipstitch Applique** | Textile paint – **Black Gold** | Thread – **Cream** | Knots – **Inside** **P. 154** Garment – Swatch—Fabric weight – **Medium** | Top-layer fabric – **Natural** | Bottom-layer fabric – **White** | Stencil – **Magdalena** | Treatment – **Negative Reverse Applique** | Textile paint – **White** | Thread – **Cream** | Knots – **Outside**

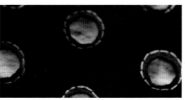

P. 157 Garment – Swatch—Fabric weight – **Medium** | Top-layer fabric – **Natural Blue Gray** | Bottom-layer fabric – **Natural Blue Gray** | Stencil – **Medium Polka Dots** | Treatment – **Featherstitch Negative Reverse Applique** | Textile paint – **Nickel** | Thread – **Gray** | Knots – **Inside** **P. 158** Garment – Swatch—Fabric weight – **Medium** | Top-layer fabric – **Black** | Bottom-layer fabric – **Faded Dots** | Stencil – **Small Polka Dots** | Treatment – **Backstitch Reverse Applique** | Textile paint – **White Gold** | Embroidery floss – **Black Varigated** | Knots – **Inside** **P.159** Garment – Swatch—Fabric weight – **Medium** | Top-layer fabric – **Ballet** | Bottom-layer fabric – **Ballet** | Stencil – **Large Polka Dots** | Treatment – **Featherstitch Negative Reverse Applique** | Textile paint – **Ecru** | Thread – **Tan** | Knots – **Inside**

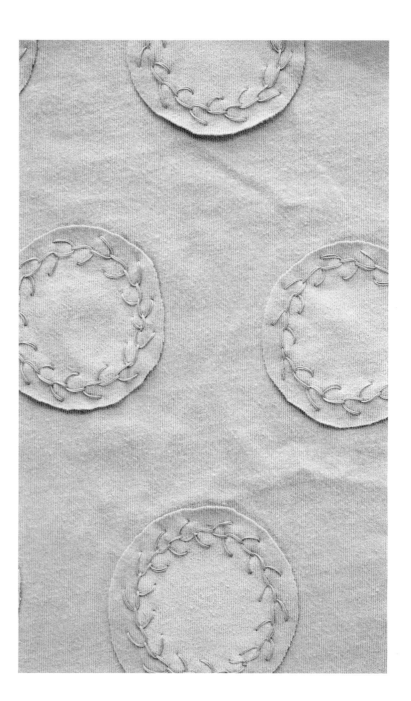

APPROXIMATE YARDAGE REQUIRED FOR BASIC GARMENTS AND ACCESSORIES

GARMENTS + ACCESSORIES	SOURCE	SINGLE LAYER	DOUBLE LAYER
Swing Skirt	Alabama Stitch Book	1 yard (.9 m)	2 yards (1.8 m)
Corset	Alabama Stitch Book	1 yard (.9 m)	2 yards (1.8 m)
Alabama Shawl	Alabama Stitch Book	1 yard (.9 m)	2 yards (1.8 m)
Camisole Top	Alabama Studio Style	1 yard (.9 m)	2 yards (1.8 m)
Camisole Tunic	Alabama Studio Style	2 yards (1.8 m)	4 yards (3.6 m)
Camisole Dress	Alabama Studio Style	3 yards (2.7 m)	6 yards (5.5 m)
Tank Top	Alabama Studio Style	1 yard (.9 m)	2 yards (1.8 m)
Tank Tunic	Alabama Studio Style	2 yards (1.8 m)	4 yards (3.6 m)
Tank Dress	Alabama Studio Style	3 yards (2.7 m)	6 yards (5.5 m)
Gore Skirt	Alabama Studio Style	2 yards (1.8 m)	4 yards (3.6 m)
Alabama Scarf	Alabama Studio Style	$\frac{1}{4}$ yard (23 cm)	$\frac{1}{2}$ yard (46 cm)
T-Shirt Top: Sleeveless, Cap, or Short Sleeves	AL Studio Sewing + Design	1 yard (.9 m)	2 yards (1.8 m)
T-Shirt Top: Long Sleeves	AL Studio Sewing + Design	2 yards (1.8 m)	4 yards (3.6 m)
Bolero: Sleeveless	AL Studio Sewing + Design	$\frac{1}{2}$ yard (46 cm)	$\frac{3}{4}$ yard (.9 m)
Bolero: Long Sleeves	AL Studio Sewing + Design	1 yard (.9 m)	2 yards (1.8 m)
Long Fitted Dress	AL Studio Sewing + Design	2 yards (1.8 m)	4 yards (3.6 m)

APPROXIMATE YARDAGE REQUIRED FOR BASIC GARMENTS AND ACCESSORIES

GARMENTS + ACCESSORIES	SOURCE	SINGLE LAYER	DOUBLE LAYER
Fitted Top	AL Studio Sewing + Design	1 yard (.9 m) or less	2 yards (1.8 m) or less
Fitted Tunic	AL Studio Sewing + Design	1 yard (.9 m)	2 yards (1.8 m)
Short Fitted Skirt	AL Studio Sewing + Design	1 yard (.9 m) or less	2 yards (1.8 m) or less
Mid-Length Fitted Skirt	AL Studio Sewing + Design	1 yard (.9 m)	2 yards (1.8 m)
Long Fitted Skirt	AL Studio Sewing + Design	1 ½ yards (1.3 m)	3 yards (2.7 m)
Poncho	AL Studio Sewing + Design	2 yards (1.8 m)	4 yards (3.6 m)
A-Line Top	AL Studio Sewing Patterns	1 yard (.9 m)	2 yards (1.8 m)
A-Line Tunic	AL Studio Sewing Patterns	1 ½ yards (1.3 m)	3 yards (2.7 m)
A-Line Dress	AL Studio Sewing Patterns	2 yards (1.8 m)	4 yards (3.6 m)
Long A-Line Dress	AL Studio Sewing Patterns	3 yards (2.7 m)	6 yards (5.5 m)
Classic Cardigan	AL Studio Sewing Patterns	1 ½ yards (1.3 m)	3 yards (2.7 m)
Classic Jacket	AL Studio Sewing Patterns	2 yards (1.8 m)	4 yards (3.6 m)
Classic Coat	AL Studio Sewing Patterns	2 ½ yards (2 m)	5 yards (4.5 m)
Short Wrap Skirt	AL Studio Sewing Patterns	¾ yard (.9 m)	1 ½ yards (1.3 m)
Wrap Skirt	AL Studio Sewing Patterns	1 yard (.9 m)	2 yards (1.8 m)
Long Wrap Skirt	AL Studio Sewing Patterns	2 yards (1.8 m)	4 yards (3.6 m)

Note: When you alter patterns by increasing or decreasing size, length, or width of a pattern piece,
you may require more or less fabric yardage than is indicated on this chart. Adjust accordingly.

ACKNOWLEDGMENTS

First and foremost, thank you to our staff, readers, clients, patrons, and supporters. Without you, this book—and Alabama Chanin—would not be possible.

And to so many, many folks, in no particular order, who have touched my life and work in immeasurable ways.

Thank you to my everyday family: my children, Maggie and Zachariah Chanin, who have stood beside me through all; Billy Smith, Sherry Dean Smith, Myra and Jim Brown, Butch Anthony; and my grandparents, Stanley and Lucille Perkins and Aaron and Christine Smith, who nurtured the garden upon which this work is built.

And to my work family: Steven Smith, Diane Hall, Sara Martin, Olivia Sherif, Erin Stephenson, Julien Archer, Maggie Crisler, Hope Carrico, Carra-Ellen Russell, Kasey Martin, Adam Chunn, Jennifer Rausch, Lyndsie McClure, Caroline Bobo, Amber Murray, Corey tenBerge, Luda Matmuratova, all of our team at The School of Making, The Factory, and Building 14, Kay Woehle, Conrad Pitts, Terry Wylie, Lisa Patterson, Roland McKinney, The Shoals Community, and the multitude of artisans who work with us and make this—and all projects—possible.

And our extended family, who have all touched this work and my life:

Robert Rausch, Deb Wood, Devin Grosz, Sun Young Park, Chris Timmons, Martha Moran, Rinne Allen, Perri Hubbard, Abraham and Susan Rowe, Peter Stanglmayr, Angie Mosier, Cathy Bailey, Robin Petrovic, Jessamyn Hatcher, Rosanne Cash, Lisa Fox, Gael Towey, Maira Kalman, Kay Gardiner, Melany Mullens, John T. Edge, the Southern Foodways Alliance, Alice Waters, Marsha Guerreo, Eva Whitechapel, Sissi Farassat, Lisa and Jess Morphew, Jessica Turner, Tom Hendrix, Katy and K.P. McNeil, Billy Reid, and all the team at Billy Reid, Eileen Fisher, Lexus, Nest, the Council of Fashion Designers of America, *Vogue* magazine, Sally Singer, Julie Gilhart, Paul Graves and former partners, Paul Kelly and Paul McKevitt for a lovely beginning.

Melanie Falick, our editor, who made this book a reality.

I am grateful eternally to one and all.

Natalie Chanin is the founder and creative director of Alabama Chanin, a lifestyle company that produces and sells well-designed and thoughtfully made goods for the person and the home. Her work with Alabama Chanin is rooted in the tenets of the Slow Design movement, which encourages designers, artists, and consumers to create and utilize thoughtful products in a socially and environmentally responsible way. She has spent a decade establishing her community of makers and educators, working to elevate and merge design, craft, and fashion.

Natalie Chanin and the work of Alabama Chanin have been featured in *Vogue*, the *New York Times*, the *Wall Street Journal*, and *Town and Country*, and on CBS News and National Public Radio. Chanin is a member of the Council of Fashion Designers of America. She is also the author of *Alabama Stitch Book*, *Alabama Studio Style*, and *Alabama Studio Sewing + Design*.

For more information about Alabama Chanin and The School of Making, to register for a workshop, or to order supplies (including project kits), visit www.alabamachanin.com/theschoolofmaking. You can also contact us via email (office@alabamachanin.com) or phone (+1.256.760.1090).

Library of Congress Control Number: 2014942995

ISBN: 978-1-61769-136-2

Editor: Melanie Falick
Technical Editor: Chris Timmons
Designer: Deb Wood and Devin Grosz
Production Manager: True Sims

Printed and bound in China
10 9 8 7 6 5 4 3

Abrams books are available at special discounts when purchased in quantity for premiums and promotions as well as fundraising or educational use. Special editions can also be created to specification. For details, contact specialsales@abramsbooks.com or the address below.

ABRAMS The Art of Books
115 West 18th Street, New York, NY 10011
abramsbooks.com